LOUIS JOLLIET

EXPLORER OF RIVERS

LOUIS JOLLIET

EXPLORER OF RIVERS

BY

VIRGINIA S. EIFERT

With maps by James Macdonald

DODD, MEAD & COMPANY
NEW YORK, 1961

This book is dedicated to all those
who know and love the rivers of America

INTRODUCTION

THIS IS THE STORY OF A MAN whose fame is written in the annals of American history, yet whose life, before and after the event which made him famous, is little known. He is Louis Jolliet who, with Father Jacques Marquette, in 1673 came down the Wisconsin River and found the Mississippi. They were the first white men to explore this unknown watercourse. It is Jolliet's and Marquette's claim to immortality.

But Louis Jolliet had lived twenty-eight eventful years before he reached the Mississippi, and, by the time he had lived twenty-seven more, he had explored widely elsewhere and become one of the most noted men of his day.

Few details about him were set down at the time. Most of the facts have been uncovered in letters written in his behalf by authorities in Canada to the King of France and his ministers, as well as in court records, documents, and in two of Jolliet's own vivid journals. It is a great and irreparable loss that his Mississippi River journal was tragically destroyed. It could have revealed much about the man and the river and its people.

Many of the documents and records from which the material in this book was obtained were brought to light and compiled by the late Jean Delanglez, S.J., Professor of His-

tory at Loyola University, Chicago, and from volumes of the
Jesuit Relations.

There is no known portrait of Louis Jolliet. Perhaps there
were no painters in Canada at the time. Even if there were,
one had to be very wealthy to afford such a service. Jolliet
was never rich; he was constantly plagued by insufficient
income.

Therefore, one may only guess at the physical characteristics of this man whom people instinctively seemed to like
and admire. Judging from the general physical attributes of
those settling in Québec in the early days—they were largely
from the west of France—some general idea may be gained
to throw light on the puzzle. The men of western France
were usually rather stocky, short, and wiry, had gray or
brown eyes, and dark hair; they were strong men who were
well equipped to combat wilderness and Indians in the New
World.

Most of the women were dark-haired and dark-eyed, often
very pretty in their youth and inclined to stoutness as they
grew older. They had long black lashes, heavy dark brows,
and fresh, rosy complexions—strong, vivacious women to
work with their men, to bear many children, and endure
the rigors of the north. It is with these general characteristics
in mind that one must visualize the Jolliets and their neighbors on the shores of the St. Lawrence and along the rivers
of the wilderness.

There has, in past years, been some confusion as to the
correct spelling of the Jolliet name. For a long time it was
given as "Joliet." A town in Illinois, named in honor of the
explorer who camped near there long ago, bears this spelling.
But in no known authentic signature did Louis Jolliet ever
sign his name in this manner. His father wrote it "Jollyet";
descendants of his brother Adrien changed it to "Joliette,"

now the name of a Canadian town. But Louis spelled it "Jolliet," always. This is the accepted spelling today.

When the Governor and the Intendant of Canada wrote about him to the King, they wrote it thus. A map, however, which purports to be his but was evidently copied by someone else, or at least the inscription copied, is not in Jolliet's handwriting; but it is signed "Joliet." Here, perhaps, the error in spelling was begun, to be compounded by later history.

In the following pages lies the story of this man whom adventure sought and fame courted, who began as a child of an obscure wheelwright living along the St. Lawrence River, in the year 1645.

CONTENTS

LOUIS JOLLIET

EXPLORER OF RIVERS

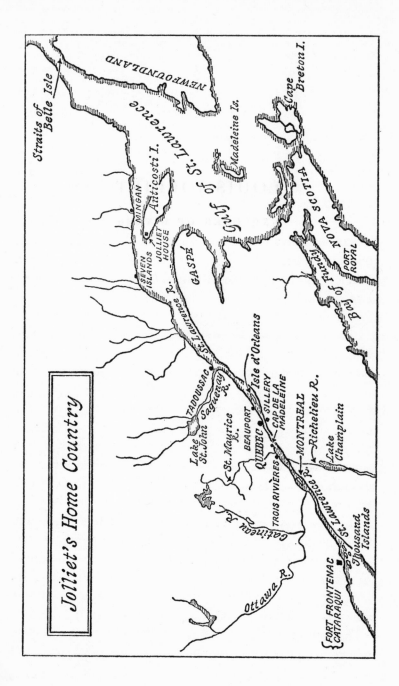

Jolliet's Home Country

1

~~~~~~

THE CHRISTENING

IT WAS HIS FIRST JOURNEY. Dressed in a simple christening robe and wrapped lovingly in a soft shawl to keep off any chilliness in the glowing autumn day, the baby alternately slept and woke as his mother hurried with the others in the little party along the north bank of the St. Lawrence River.

It was September 21, 1645, and Jean and Marie Jolliet were taking their newest-born son to Québec for baptism. They had left their sturdy log and stone house which faced the river at Beauport two miles below the city and, with their other two children and several friends, had set off early for the church. As they walked, maple leaves were scarlet and yellow above them, or lay in a gaudy carpet under their feet. The river had a glitter where a growing wind whipped up cross-currents and white-capped wavelets, while, far up the stream, Québec lay dim and indistinct on its hilltop.

The men went ahead. Jean Jolliet, blue knitted cap jaunty on his head, loose blouse and woolen trousers topped with a broad, thick, red-and-blue twisted wool sash tied around the waist, carried little Marie. Until the new baby had been born, Marie, now two years old, had been the baby. Adrien, who was five, trotted happily at his father's side.

The Jolliets' neighbor, Robert Giffard, an eminent surgeon and the seigneur of Beauport, strode along with Jean and

1

placidly smoked his pipe. Just behind them, carrying a netted bag containing the lunch, plodded the silent Louis Maheu. He was to be the baby's godfather. Jean and Robert now and again turned to say something to him, but Louis Maheu, though a faithful friend, never talked much and it was a one-sided conversation at best.

Marie d'Abancourt Jolliet and her husband had come as children from the west of France; they had been married in Québec. Today in honor of the coming event she was dressed in her best full-skirted black gown with lace fichu; she wore a cap stiff with starched lace. Françoise Giffard, Robert's daughter, wore a pretty blue gown whose billowing skirts switched in the breeze as she walked, and now and again caught against a bramble in the path. On her curly black hair was her handsomest lace cap, securely tied down to keep it on her head in the river wind. Though she was only eleven years old, Françoise Giffard wore a certain pride and womanly dignity which belied her few years, for she who was still only a child was betrothed and would be married within two months.

Françoise and Marie talked together of the marriage plans. Adrien lagged a moment to pitch a stone into the river. The men argued about the fishing and the state of affairs in Québec. As they proceeded they could see the town on the cliff growing more distinct, could make out the forms of houses and chimney smokes atop the gray headland. At the base, the harbor was marked with the masts of ships lying at anchor and, in the lowland, the ramshackle houses and warehouses standing about the stone fort which Champlain had erected years before.

But it was still dim and misted and seemed farther away than it really was. Over all that landscape dominated by the river, by the Laurentian mountains on the horizon, and by the multicolored autumn leaves against the dark green of spruces, there lay a thin blue veiling of autumn haze. It blurred the colors, obscured a clear view of the city, merged sky with river, so that everything on that lovely day took on an almost dreamlike look, unreal and far and without substance to the people coming toward the town.

The way was really not long. They were soon at the bank of the St. Charles River separating them from where the now towering headland stood beyond. While they waited for the small ferryboat, they could see the houses clearly, could easily recognize this roof and that barn. They discussed it all with the mounting excitement of having come in from the edge of wilderness to this place which was the only approximation of a city in the neglected land of New France.

Taking advantage of the chance to sit down in the ferry, Marie opened her dress so that while she rested the baby could nurse. When they were at last across the river and in the dusty, rutted streets of the lower town, the long steep climb up Mountain Hill still confronted them. Marie Jolliet, strong young Frenchwoman though she was, had nevertheless given birth to a child only two weeks before, and had found that the walk in from Beauport had been more tiring than she would admit. Now, as if it towered to the sky, the hill seemed insurmountable. But the church was at the top, and the others had already started ahead, so Marie took a deep breath, held the wrapped baby against her bosom, and set off to catch up with the rest of the party, already halfway along the incline.

But Robert Giffard with a smile turned back, removed the infant from his mother's weary arms, and carried the bundle up the steeps while Marie, with renewed strength, came after them.

The top of the hill gave them a marvelous view of the great St. Lawrence and the way along which they had just come. It was a sight to invigorate the weariest soul. They now stood together with feeling of triumph on the crest of the very headland which had been their horizon and goal for several hours. They could see the distant mountains even better than from below, felt an awe to behold the tremendous waters of the river blurring in autumn haze and glittering to the eastward, to merge with the gulf and the far-off sea. They could look down on the harbor and see rooftops and the ships in from France, could see sailors on the decks and cargoes of furs being loaded. These ships were soon to start back across the Atlantic on a long voyage which, with luck, would get them home by the time winter had set in—that is if, without adequate navigation maps, the pilots even got the ships safely out of the dangerous river itself. There would be no more vessels coming up to Québec until late next spring.

It was always a wrench to the Canadians to see the last ship going back to France, a feeling almost of bereavement, of desertion, of momentary panic. With the ships gone and the river a mass of immobile, savage ice, the great violence of the northern winter a reality to be fought with for survival, and the Iroquois drawing an implacable net of hatred around them, anything could happen in Québec, and no one in France would be the wiser.

Since it was almost midday and the walk had been long, they decided to pause here on the cliff's rim. While they enjoyed the view and rested, they could eat. Louis Maheu opened the bag he had carried all the way and laid a white napkin on the rock to serve as a tablecloth. He got out the dark bread, the cheese, the onions, and a bottle of wine. Holding the loaf against his chest, he carefully cut thick chunks and laid them on the napkin. He sliced the onions, averting his face while his eyes watered. Then each person hacked off a piece of cheese to put on his bread and onion, and washed it all down with wine from the bottle.

When the last crumb had been eaten and the final drop drunk, the group went more briskly along the dusty street where they continually found something to stop and look at, with appropriate exclamations. They stared at some of the fine stone houses and looked into gardens in which flowers and bean vines lay blackened by the recent frost. Jean Jolliet greeted men he knew. Now and again a passing oxcart sent the group back against a wall. They all gave reverent greetings to a Jesuit with a basket of turnips from the seminary garden, and to a pair of nuns hurrying on silent feet to the convent of the Ursulines. Several times the whole party had to halt patiently while Marie proudly showed her infant to a friend on her doorstep.

Finally, at the corner of Ste Anne and Des Jardins Streets, they came to the long, log-and-timbered, two-story building which was the House of the One Hundred Associates, headquarters for the fur company which controlled and profited by all the trade in Canada. Jean Jolliet himself was employed by the company as wagonmaker and wheelwright. His friend, François Bissot, who worked there, too, waited with his family outside the building for the Jolliets to arrive.

They had gathered in the sunshine under the golden maples—the Bissots with their year-old infant, and Mme Guillaumette Couillard, Marie Bissot's mother, as well as some of the numerous Couillard children.

On the second floor of this imposing building a room for some time had been used as a church. Lamentably for all in that parish, the beautiful cathedral of Notre Dame de la Recouvrance, built by the illustrious Champlain to celebrate the return of the French to Québec in 1632, had been burned to the ground in 1640, and as yet nothing had been done to rebuild it. This was the result of apathy as well as lack of money; some said that the authorities never seemed to care much nowadays about what happened in Québec. The colony, in fact, was falling to pieces through lack of interest and initiative both here and in France. And so, for want of a better religious edifice, the Jesuits for the time being had been given the use of the lower floor of the House of One Hundred Associates, while an upper room had been converted to a chapel.

The Bissots and Mme Couillard greeted the Jolliets and the others with exclamations of joy and affection. The volatile François clapped Jean on the shoulders, kissed him loudly on both cheeks and was paid back in kind, all in a sort of bearlike dance, while he congratulated his friend on having been man enough to produce another son.

Marie Bissot and Marie Jolliet kissed and cried out in delight at seeing one another again. Mme Couillard saluted the new mother and turned back the edge of the shawl around the baby to exclaim over his sweet sleeping face. Her daughter and the younger children wanted to see, too, and the two little boys who had been scuffling like puppies in the fallen leaves had to be lifted up for a look. There was a fine ado in the street. Finally François shouted impatiently to leave off the gabbling and come at once. They must all get about the business of assuring this child a legal name and a place in heaven before he was an hour older. The good Father Vimont would of a surety decide that they were all heathens with no regard for the soul of this hapless infant.

So Jean and François clumped noisily up the creaking stairs to the second floor. They were followed by Louis Maheu and the more sedate Dr. Giffard. At all the commotion the baby woke up. Some of the Jesuits came out of their door to greet the party as the women finally rounded up all the children and got them started up the stairs. Several other friends, aunts, and cousins were already sitting on the unpadded wooden seats or kneeling on the splintery prayer benches.

The chapel was only a makeshift place for services. It was not a spacious room, but then neither was the parish a large one. There were, besides, two other churches to fill the spiritual needs of the rest of Québec and its environs. The chapel was so small, in fact, that midnight mass could be celebrated with only four candles, but this was considered to be quite a sufficient reverence and illumination, and besides, candles were costly. In the wilderness of New France one could not be as prodigal of precious candlewax, even for the glory of God, as in France where there was a beehive behind every rural home and in every convent garden.

Yet this room, sanctified by the Holy Spirit, nevertheless held the quiet atmosphere of a church. It smelled of incense; and blending with this was the gentle odor of wax in the votive lights flickering at the feet of the Blessed Virgin. The scent of weathering pine in the broad boards of floor and wall brought the smell of the out-of-doors, while between the cracks came the commingled aroma of stored furs, seal oil, dried codfish, and other items in the Company's warehouse below.

But it was the essence of the forest whose perfume and whose influence were strongest here, the forest which was never too far away from anyone along the river. The forest held an inescapable warning, was an ever-present part of the life of these people of New France. While it often terrified them and sometimes brought their deaths, the presence of the trees themselves was an assurance almost as comforting as the church itself.

One could not think of this land without the forest that mantled the landscape as far as the distant Laurentians rising purple on the horizon; without the spruce forests growing more ragged and sparse beyond the mountains toward

the land where the Mistasinnis lived; or without the pines
growing ever greater on the other side of the river, into the
mountains of the Mohawks and the English. But though the
forest gave life to Canada—gave maple sugar and furs and
lumber and meat—a man had to be strong to contend with
the forces of evil which it held and which seemed per-
petually bent upon challenging and, if possible, destroying
him. Enemy of civilization, the antithesis to culture, yet this
wilderness was mother to it and inescapable from its course
in the New World.

Every person gathered in this church had been affected
by the forest, would be influenced by it as long as he or she
would live, and some here present would lose their lives in
it. Dangerous, beautiful, violent, the wilderness lured men
in spite of themselves. Father Vimont and his brother Jesuits
had seen with despair how the strong, exuberant, dark-
browed young Frenchmen, coming to Canada, seemed to
be injected by it with a reckless disregard for the laws of
king and France and colony. The forest called many of them,
and they were never the same afterward. Not all were faithful to church and family; many never returned to civilization
but took Indian wives and refused obedience to church and
state. It was easier, one of the clergy wrote sadly, "to make
an Indian out of a Frenchman, than a Frenchman out of an
Indian."

For out there to the westward beneath interlocking boughs
of trees which the people in the church could see from the
windows, a man could walk free and wild and beholden to no
one but himself, and neither king nor priest could find him
there; that is, if he chose not to be found. He could go on
forever, from the Saguenay to the setting sun. And who knew
where the forest ended, if it ever did, before reaching the
Great South Sea?

Father Vimont knew how it was with these men. He had

known the siren call of the forest himself. Now, in his black
gown and lace-edged surplice, he came into the dim church,
and the people knelt with a rustling of skirts and scraping of
shoes.

Mme Bissot and her mother had taken charge of the Jolliet
children, along with the Bissot infant himself and the young
and exuberant Couillards. Marie Bissot was the capable and
energetic granddaughter of the honored Louis Hébert, first
settler and physician of Québec, and a person of conse-
quence and character. Like her mother she was an attractive, forceful woman who had married very young and had,
at the mature age of twelve years, begun a family which
would eventually number eleven sturdy and handsome children.

The prayer was already finished when Marie Bissot's sister,
Marguerite, slipped into a seat at the back. She was just
past twenty years old and for three years had been the
widow of the explorer, Jean Nicolet. Unlike many young
widows in New France, who frequently took another husband
almost immediately after the death of the first, Marguerite
Nicolet had not remarried; her memories of the splendid
man who had so briefly been her husband were still too vivid
to be replaced by another.

Father Vimont began the sacrament of holy baptism.
Little Françoise Giffard, her dark eyes very solemn, performed with credit her part as godmother. Louis Maheu, who
had forgotten to remove his cap until Jean nudged his ribs,
muttered the right responses at the proper times, and the
holy oil was marked upon the small brow of the wide-eyed
baby. The child did not disgrace his family by crying, and
was at last duly baptized and entered on the church register
as Louis Jolliet.

The blessing pronounced, Jean shook hands with the priest

and with the godfather and François Bissot and Robert Giffard. Mlle Giffard handed over the infant to his mother, and the whole party from Beauport set off again down the steep street toward the river. They wanted to reach home before the early autumn dusk set in. With the Iroquois so touchy of late, it was just as well to get indoors before nightfall.

Perhaps it was significant that this new baby on his first journey should have been carried along the St. Lawrence, and that one of the first things he would see when he could lift his head and look about him would be that great, challenging, gray-blue expanse of river passing his home in Beauport, coming from some unknown source on its way to the distant sea.

For the river and the waters from which it flowed in the western wilderness were the key to the story of America which was to begin unfolding in his lifetime, and in which he would play an unforgettable part. The waters which were the vital lifeline of the French in their grim struggle for life on the northeast rim of an unknown continent were the crux of this new child's destiny.

But on that autumn evening in 1645, Louis Jolliet, his dark head quiet against the pillow in his cradle, slept.

2

~~~~~

THE WAY WEST

Louis Jolliet came into the world at a time when the people of Québec were reaching a low ebb of discouragement and fear. The town, begun in 1608, was still poorly developed. Although there were some good stone houses, many more were still made of logs, and no one seemed interested in improving them. The crooked, haphazard streets were unpaved, industries were almost nonexistent, agriculture feeble, shipping meager. The only acceptable livelihood, in the opinion of most Québec men, was the fur trade, but with the Iroquois so irritable and so great a menace of late, even the fur trade was languishing.

Much of the blame was placed on the failure of the Company of One Hundred Associates to fulfill the pact made when Cardinal Richelieu and Louis XIII gave it the trading rights in Canada, in exchange for protection of the struggling colony and for development of towns and farms. The Company had profited well enough from furs brought in when great fleets of hundreds of Indian canoes came out of the wilderness in summer, bringing pelts trapped and stretched during the previous winter in remote Indian country to the north and west. While the Indians remained tolerably friendly and came to the trading fairs at Tadoussac, Trois Rivières, and Montréal, largely because of their insatiable thirst for French brandy obtainable here when the trading was done, the French seldom had to go out to get their furs. And half the profits had usually been sent, according to the agreement, to the King. After a while less than the full portion went across the sea, then less and less, while dismal reports of failing business accompanied the meager profits.

In its oftentimes shady career in Canada, the Company of One Hundred Associates had not been particularly solicitous of the welfare of the people in New France. Little effort was made to improve living conditions or build permanent homes or businesses; protection against hostile tribes was scant or nonexistent. It was said scornfully that the Company did not know how to cope with savages, but hid behind the skirts of the priests who were going out as missionaries to the Indians and were largely protected by their own sanctity and selfless purposes.

The people of Canada, numbering fewer than two thousand when Louis Jolliet was born into a situation which was far from hopeful, were sick of failure and disaster. Many wanted to go back to France where life, though hard, at least was predictable, and where one had not the daily chance of dying horribly at the hand of a savage. But families could not return without the King's permission, and he would not give it. Besides, they had sold everything when they departed for the New World, and really had little to which to return.

It had all begun there along the St. Lawrence when, in 1535, Jacques Cartier had sailed his three ships into the mouth of an unknown river leading from a great gulf lying beyond Newfoundland. He had worked his way cautiously four hundred miles upstream, found friendly Indians, and stayed there all winter when his ships were frozen in the ice. Cartier returned twice more to Canada, each time exploring more territory in the name of the King, but going away again without leaving any tangible settlement.

Not until Samuel de Champlain came in 1608, after having explored a thousand miles inland up the St. Lawrence from the sea, did any town begin to rise. Champlain built a fort in the lowland beneath a great gray headland in the place he called Québec. Thirty-six years later another settlement began to grow in the wilderness 167 miles upstream, on an island with a mountain in its center, called Montréal.

At first only a few men brought their families to Québec. Canada was too dangerous a venture, held too uncertain a fate for women and children. When news of a wealth to be had in beaver furs reached France, however, many men came out to Canada with the idea of making a quick fortune and then returning to France to spend it where money had some meaning. Although the King, almost by force, insisted that people should come to Québec, few men wanted to stay long enough or work hard enough to accomplish even the elusive bubble of ordinary comfort as represented in a good home and a garden. They came for fish and furs and whatever treasure they might pick up. They were traders, trappers, hunters, fishermen, criminals, and fools—and not many of these had the stamina, the wish, or the ideals to stay and build a city with Champlain.

But the King sent a family in 1617 who warmed Champlain's heart and renewed his faith in men. Louis Hébert was a physician and apothecary who had been ordered to America to minister to the ills of the people. With a wife and three children and his household goods, Louis Hébert came to stay. He and his family expected to build as good a life in New France as they had had in Paris, if not an even better one. Therefore, they brought with them not only furniture and clothing and medicines, but garden seeds, several cocks and hens, an ox, a cow, and a couple of pigs.

Instead of settling in the more dismal area of the lower town, Louis Hébert cleared ten acres of land on top of the rock, where he built a fine stone house and laid out a farm. He added to his livestock when later ships came from France, and soon had a flock of sheep which produced the first wool in the colony, a delightful commodity in this cold country. The Héberts did so well with their crops that they were soon feeding a good many of the less provident people of Québec.

Champlain, wishing he had a hundred like the Héberts, was thankful for these good people, not only for their industry and optimism, but for their company. Many an evening he climbed the steep Mountain Hill to the summit of the rock for a long talk with Hébert and his wife. It was a great grief when the former was killed in a fall on the ice in January, 1627.

Slowly, somehow, Québec was growing. By 1629, courage was increasing. People were looking forward to the three supply ships coming out with new colonists and with supplies which would see Québec through another winter. There was no warning that trouble, and not the supply ships, was approaching up the river.

The Kirke brothers had captured the three vessels when they passed Tadoussac below Québec.

The English for many years had largely ignored the French far away in the north, and at the time there was no real war between the two, though the ancient enmity was always present. The Kirkes, however, had been given letters of marque by Charles I of England to do what they could in wiping out the French from Québec. Certainly the most drastic blow they could have planned was to waylay the supply ships when there was no time for more to come to Québec before winter.

Nevertheless, when Champlain was requested to surren-

der, he refused. The Kirkes, apparently acceding to his refusal, sailed away, but they took with them the three supply
ships and the colonists who were aboard. And thereupon
began the long siege of hunger which was worse than bom-
bardments of cannon. Winter grew hungrier. Long before
spring, the people were reduced to starvation rations.

When springtime came, the survivors went out to the
woods to dig roots, to salvage anything that lived, while
hardly a rat or a cat remained uneaten in the town.

When Champlain and his people were at their lowest ebb,
the Kirke brothers sailed back and demanded the surrender
which now could not but be given. The triumphant con-
querors, who had used hunger as a bitter weapon, ordered
Champlain and the other officials, and the priests and nuns
and many of the people, to return to France. Madame Hébert
and her children, however, begged to be allowed to remain.
This was home. They wished no other.

Three years passed. Life in the all-but-deserted wilderness atop the rock of Québec was grim and without much
hope, only a tenacious holding on with the trust that someday France would return to Canada. And in France, Samuel
de Champlain could not forget Québec, the river, the Héberts, or the ever-alluring wilderness whose mysteries he
had not solved. He must go back. And then it was suddenly
made possible. In 1632, when European politics changed,
the French were free to go back to Canada.

Ships set out, Champlain's in the lead, eager to get home
again. Supplies, people, and hope went with him. And so
one fine summer day, when Mme Hébert went to the door
to shake out a tablecloth she was transfixed, with the white
cloth in her hands, at what she saw coming up the river
from around the Île d'Orléans. Ships!

Her gasp brought her children and grandchildren to the

door. They ran down the garden to the lane and to the cliff edge to watch in dreadful anxiety for what should come next. They could not at a distance perceive what flags flew above the billowing sails; it might be the English come back again, and God only knew what indignities and horrors they might not wreak.

But then they saw the lovely lily banners of France—the snowy field with the three golden fleur-de-lis glinting in the sunshine. Mme Hébert, who still gripped the tablecloth, now lifted it in the air and waved it frantically while tears ran down her face. Everyone was weeping as the ships reached port at last. The people who had been left behind in the ruined lower town gathered at the waterfront, mute now, devouring the French ships and sailors with their long-denied eyes and hearts.

All those who could offered shelter to the newcomers until fresh habitations should be built, but the Héberts insisted that to their house and to none other should come the Jesuits, the Ursulines, and Champlain himself until his own house should be repaired.

In the Hébert home, with its altar where family prayers had been so fervent and so desperate for many years, the Jesuits held their first services. People who could not crowd into the house listened from the windows.

Father Le Jeune, one of the returned priests, wrote:

> When they saw our ships coming in with white flags upon the masts, they knew not how to express their joy. But when they saw us in their home, to celebrate the holy Mass, which they had not heard for three years, Good God, what joy! Tears fell from the eyes of nearly all, so great was their happiness.

Champlain and the Church had come back. A new vigor pulsed through Québec. He set about at once to rebuild the city. It was he who erected the new cathedral which he named Notre Dame de la Recouvrance to celebrate the return.

Always while he labored on his renewed city, Champlain pondered on the mystery of the rivers. He had, indeed, followed the St. Lawrence a long distance inland, but had nowhere reached the end of the connecting waterways which apparently stretched interminably to the west. Long before the Kirkes' invasion, he had heard the Indians speak of fresh-water seas extending even farther westward beyond the river, to an even bigger water.

To the eager French, this news could only mean one thing: out there to the west lay the Pacific Ocean, the Vermilion Sea, the Great South Sea, whatever one wanted to call it, the link of French commerce with the treasures of the Orient. The French, the English, the Dutch, and the Spanish had been contesting since the discovery of the New World to be first to find the coveted short route to China. To be first —but a continent lay between New France and the Pacific, how wide a land they did not know. Yet they felt as certain as if it were some hidden knowledge born into their brains and only to be uncovered when the time was right and the mystery solved that there was indeed a way through the continent to the west, some inside passage, a water route to the far sea through the trackless wilderness of New France.

The St. Lawrence had seemed to be the logical and obvious route. It had been Champlain's first certainty when he came to America. He was positive that it must lead to the Pacific. The river split a continent in a great schism that narrowed to a fork above the island of Montréal. Here from the northwest came the rapids of the Ottawa River, while the lower fork, the St. Lawrence itself, passed among many green islands that were like a fleet of viridian ships. Past the islands, the river widened suddenly into the fresh-water lake called Ontario that looked as wide as a sea.

It was said that another river came into the far end of this lake, by way of a great waterfall, and connected with still another lake above, but there was no way of knowing how far these linking waters went, for no white man had gone to find out. No one knew whence the Ottawa flowed, either. The forest apparently went on forever and so, evidently, did the watercourses.

During Champlain's early years in Canada, he had become profoundly aware that it was the lack of understanding of the Indians on the part of the French which held back or thwarted any attempt to explore and discover the land to the west. The hostility of the Indians and the futility of trying to understand their unknown tongues, as much as the physical dangers of the wilderness itself, prevented the French from finding out what they wanted to know. Not only had Cartier, long ago, infuriated the Indians, but Champlain himself had compounded many further insults on the Iroquois and neighboring tribes. The Iroquois themselves were a proud and intolerant people who responded to insults with outrage and murder, and very soon had gone over to ally themselves with the English south of the river. Angering the Iroquois had been a costly mistake on the part of the French, a mistake for which France and Canada and many innocent people were to pay in blood and bitterness for more than a century.

Champlain knew that before Frenchmen might safely penetrate the wilderness or set colonies farther westward, he must send men of good will out to learn about the people, not all of whom were hostile but who could be wrongly influenced by the Iroquois or the English unless the French got to them first and made them their friends. Only through friendship and tact, Champlain was belatedly deciding, could he hope to find the way to solving the northern mystery, the urgent whereabouts of the great sea and the way to China.

Long before the attack of the English in 1629, he had begun to remedy this situation. Young Jean Nicolet had come to Canada in the service of Champlain, who saw in him one of the diplomats he was seeking to improve relations with the Indians. Nicolet was thereupon sent out to live with the Algonquins and learn their language and habits, to be one of them and find out how the Indians thought and lived. And Jean Nicolet, with only a few returns back to civilization, spent fourteen years in the northern wilderness.

He had been up the Ottawa River in 1629 when the English attacked Québec, but remote though he was from contact with his people, the news of what had happened reached him even there. Indians brought information in relays, one canoeman passing on the word to another all the way up the Ottawa. When Nicolet heard of the tragedy at Québec, he could hardly believe it. Champlain was strong and powerful; France itself was invincible. Yet the Indians vowed it was so, and that the great Onontio and his people had gone away from Québec.

It had been too late to be of help. With his people leaving Canada, Nicolet's whole life now lay with his adopted people of the forest. He went away from the Algonquin town at last and traveled still farther up into a country which was greatly distant from all French and English contact, where no white man had ever gone before him, and there he lived among the Hurons. He had almost ceased by that time to feel like a Frenchman. It was while he was with the Hurons that he discovered where the Ottawa River went, and how one could portage to Lake Nipissing and thence

to the next river, which he named the French River in honor
of his people. This led eventually into one of the upper
Great Lakes, to which no white man had ever come before
. . . Lake Huron.

Three years later he heard the news that the old governor
was back and that the French had returned to Québec. It
was time, Nicolet knew, for him to go home.

He scarcely recognized the renewed Québec, or the
changed spirit of the people. Sturdy houses of gray stone
and timber replaced the mud and log huts and the burned
ruins left by the siege. More important now, a different class
of people was coming. Every ship brought them, people
who would stay and build. Around the Hébert land and
home other houses of substance were being built and more
land cleared. Streets were laid out in the upper town around
the new cathedral. A street replaced the muddy path which
climbed from the lower town to the upper.

Québec with its narrow, angular streets and the com-
fortingly familiar French-style stone-and-timber houses, the
sounds and smells of the town, and the sight of ships in the
harbor, all must have looked wonderfully civilized to Nicolet
after his years in the lodges of the Hurons and the Algonquins, after his years in the free and fragrant forests.

Champlain, an aging man of sixty-five, had felt that Nicolet had surely long since perished in the wilderness. The
old governor wept with as much joy as if a son had been
returned to him that day, when the sun-browned Nicolet,
looking like an Indian, took the steps two at a time in mounting to Champlain's rooms in the new Chateau St. Louis, to
embrace his old friend. Nicolet's youthful vigor instilled in
Champlain a renewed energy of his own. The two sat over
many plans, night after night by candlelight in the chateau.

Champlain put Nicolet to work as an interpreter and
Indian agent in the new town of Trois Rivières, a busy

trading station which had sprung up betwen Québec and Montréal. He spoke with the Indians who came to trade. He could deal with them better than anyone else and was relied upon by Indian and French alike to keep matters on an even keel between the two peoples. It was from one of the Indians coming to the post that he heard something strange which he relayed promptly to the governor.

Far to the west, Nicolet related with excitement, the Indian had said there was a people who were different from the Hurons and Montagnais and Iroquois. They had broad, flat faces and their skins were not so much copper-red as almost as yellow as a pumpkin. They were called the Salt People, the People of the Sea.

As he spoke, he saw how the governor's interest seethed with some of the enthusiasm of the old days. His tired face lit as from within; he sat forward in his chair, listening. As soon as Nicolet finished, Champlain burst forth with excitement which the old man had lacked since his exile and the destruction of Québec.

Champlain was not well. He had been, besides, in his growing age, cruelly hurt by the fact that his young wife, Hélène, had been so unhappy here with him that she had returned to France to enter the convent. Though he now existed only for Canada, the old fire had seemed to have been extinguished forever.

Nicolet knew that the same thoughts were passing through Champlain's mind as had passed immediately through his own. The Salt People, the People of the Sea, with yellow skins and flat faces—they could only mean one thing: here must be inhabitants of the edge of the Orient itself, the rim of China lying not many days' journey beyond the green and endless western horizon. The Indian had told him how to find the place across a great water which could be reached by means of the upper Ottawa and the portage to Lake Huron.

Champlain sent Nicolet out to find it. If he located the possible short route to China, it would be a great accomplishment for Champlain and would illuminate his name in history. But principally and secretly, however, Nicolet was getting himself back to the Indian country of the western wilderness for which he was desperately homesick. With one canoe and several Indians, he set off in 1634. He would not mind how hard the way might be. He had been given his inner wish to go back to the wilderness.

Portaging rapids, pulling the canoe through shallows, paddling when possible, he followed the Ottawa to the northwest. For weeks he traversed wild waters that tumbled between dark forests of pine and hemlock, where long gray lichens hanging from branches mantled the trees with misty gray. The forest was so deep that only an occasional thrush voice broke the silence, and the deer watched the lone canoe and then leaped across the thick beds of moss so soft and resilient that no footfall was heard. He passed the tangles of tamarack swamps and bays in the river where moose fed muzzle-deep in water lilies. Or he saw a bear watching from some rocky point, and sometimes an Indian, too, intently scrutinizing him, then melting away into the secrecy of the alder thickets.

At last one day Nicolet, after portaging from Lake Nipissing to the French River as the Hurons had shown him, came down its shallows and into Lake Huron. He went on rapidly, hugging the island-strewn shore and passing rocky headlands and deserted sandy beaches. He rounded the quiet, rocky bulk of Michilimackinac Island brooding in the summer sun, passed through the sun-glittered rips of the Straits of Mackinac which connected Lake Huron with Lake Michigan. No white man had ever been here before.

Pines stood aloof and dark and silent above the shore. A fragrance of warm needles in the sun filled the quiet, warm air. This remote, still, brilliant, perfumed land of the Great Lakes was an almost overwhelming spiritual as well as physical experience. But dominating all was the urgent wish to satisfy Champlain's dearest longing for America—to find at last the way to China. Thus far Nicolet had certainly seen nothing that would lead anyone to think he had gone so far; and certainly there was no salt water. Not yet. One great fresh-water lake seemed to open into another. Where was the sea? Where were the Salt People?

His Indian companions paddled the canoe steadily down the west shore of Lake Michigan into a bay formed by a long white limestone peninsula. Over the cliffs were draped dark green arborvitae trees; wind-wracked forest stood erect behind the windbreak. The bay—Green Bay—narrowed. The canoe obediently followed its contours along the peninsula, and, as the rocky portion was left behind, he saw how waves driven by the wind had gouged out soft red-purple clay which stained the water for many rods outward, and began to leave a stain on the white bark of the canoe.

It was on the bluff above the colorful earth called Red Banks, in the place where the Indian at Trois Rivières had told him, that he saw smokes. And up the hill there were people who were silhouetted anonymously against the summer sky as they stood watching him.

His Indians shoved the canoe into the sand, and Nicolet stepped ashore. He hastily opened an oilskin-wrapped parcel and donned an elaborate velvet hat with plumes. Over his deerskin clothing he put on a long brocaded and embroidered Chinese robe. He loaded a brace of pistols and then waited, incongruously glorious in the sunshine, yet a little ridiculous, too, woodsman as he was, in this inappropriate garb. But if they were indeed the Chinese, he had reasoned, they would be impressed by finding the newcomer suitably dressed in their style.

The silhouettes moved cautiously down the hill-trail toward him. Before they had come very far, Nicolet raised his hands and fired both pistols into the air.

A crowd of gulls resting on a sandspit took off with a swirl of panicky feathers, and the hill people fell back in stunned horror. He did not reload or fire again. Enough was enough; there was no need to overdo it.

As he waited, an edge of water crept up to darken the silk of the gown's trailing hem.

As the people on the bluff came slowly toward the man in his magnificence, Jean Nicolet's spirits dropped. These were not the Chinese. By no stretch of the imagination could they be converted into Orientals, nor could this red-stained beach be called China. On the shores of the Door of Death peninsula in Wisconsin, Jean Nicolet met the friendly Winnebagoes.

He went with them to their village atop the bluff. It was too late in the summer now to start back to Québec, and, besides, he wanted to learn more about these people. The best way he knew was to live with them for a while. He spent the winter with these, the Salt People, learned their language, went out on exploring trips, and talked with visitors from other tribes who might come here. But none could tell him of any way to get to the sea. They had never heard of the sea or known what it was.

When he set forth in spring he brought back with him a canoe loaded with beaver furs of great silkiness as a present for Champlain. The old man was disappointed in the geographical implications of Nicolet's failure to find China, yet he had begun to feel that his own mission here, as well as New France's place in America, was not so much to find the way to the western sea which led to China, vital though it was, but to exploit the New World's own products and riches. Champlain sat, chin in hand, furs on his knee, eyes fixed on some distant point beyond the window, and dreamed of what would come.

Champlain gave up all his ideas of solving the northern mystery. Perhaps some day someone would do this, would find the way where the waters led and so discover the route to the Pacific which everyone sought, would learn at last the devious secrets of the Great Lakes and the rivers which dominated the middle continent, so much more huge than anyone had ever suspected. But it was not to be for him.

Several months after Nicolet's return, Champlain suffered a stroke. Paralyzed, he lay in his chill stone bedroom in the Chateau St. Louis, unable even to lift his head to look again at the St. Lawrence freezing blue-gray below the rock. Nicolet was with him day and night. Staunch friends came and went, and Mme Hébert tended him. But it was too late.

Life left him on Christmas Day, 1635.

Jean Nicolet never went back to the wilderness which he had learned to know almost as well as the Indians did, and which he loved fiercely as part of himself. He settled at Trois Rivières and was married to young Marguerite Couillard, the eleven-year-old granddaughter of Mme Hébert. His child-wife wanted him to stay near. The wilderness was too terrifyingly close around. Jean Nicolet remained at home and dealt prosaically in furs brought in by the Indians.

Now and again a familiar brown face would be there in front of him, a torrent of Huron or Algonquin. The strange gutturals would fall into place, and he would burst into a conversation that would refresh him like a cold, rushing stream in the forest. He always felt that perhaps when his wife might not mind so much, he would go back to the Indians.

There were times when they came to him not alone for furs to trade but with troubles to be solved. One winter day in 1642, an Indian prisoner in Trois Rivières needed assistance quickly, but Nicolet chanced to be away on business in Québec. An Indian messenger set off down the still unfrozen river, found him in the city, and told him that he must come at once. Nicolet wanted nothing more than this —an Indian needed him—to cause him to stop what he was doing, halt his business transactions, and leave immediately.

There were neither horses nor roads. The river was the highway. That cold evening he sailed in the only available vessel going that way on such a night, a shallop with M. de Savigny and three men as crew who were carrying the Savigny household goods to Trois Rivières, where he was moving his family. It was a wild night, unfit for any sort of vessel to be afloat, but apparently Savigny was in a hurry, and so was Nicolet. The wind grew stronger, and when the boat was not far out of Québec harbor a sudden squall from the northwest lashed the river to frenzy. Waves caught the little boat broadside. It leaped, filled, churned, turned over.

The five men clung desperately for a while to the overturned hull. In the bitter cold of the wave-lashed stormy night, their numbed hands lost their grip and one by one the men were swept into the water. Nicolet, able woodsman though he was, could not swim well enough to save himself in a wild, cold winter river such as this. M. de Savigny, clinging beside Nicolet, heard him murmur a few words, and then he was gone, vanished in the angry waters.

Savigny alone made the bank. Half dead and nearly frozen, he struggled to the Jesuit house in Sillery where he was taken in. The priests worked over him, warmed him, and he slowly revived to tell his terrible story.

There was an Indian, one of those who lived at the mission at Sillery, who heard, and he ran to tell the others. In the wind and slashing spray that night the Indians crowded lamenting to the dark shore of the St. Lawrence and, as Father Vimont wrote, "manifested unspeakable grief to see him appear no more."

There were few Frenchmen whom the Indians ever mourned, but they mourned Jean Nicolet, their friend and their brother. Their wailing chants rose to the stormy night, and, as the news passed into the forests on the days following, the chants continued along the riverways of the wilderness.

Jean Nicolet was dead in the St. Lawrence. Although he had not solved the northern mystery, he had opened the way to the west.

In 1645, three years after his death, his widow's nephew, Louis Jolliet, was born in a simple log-and-stone house above the rocky shore of the river.

3

~~~~~

THE IROQUOIS

IN THE SAME YEAR in which Louis Jolliet was born, a seven-year-old boy, also named Louis, who had been King of France for two years since the death of his father, demanded an Indian costume.

Almost everyone had heard of the ferocious Red Indians of America, of the curious customs they had, and their strange manner of dress. Louis XIII, his father, had never been very much concerned about what went on in Canada, but the boy was growing aware of it even at the age of seven. And perhaps his first awareness came with this sudden wish to dress up like an American savage.

The order was relayed by way of the next ship to Canada and carried to the long-suffering Jesuit fathers, who would be the ones most likely to have access to what the young despot wanted. The Jesuits were shocked at the request.

Knowing the Iroquois and Montagnais and Hurons as they did, the priests could not visualize the illustrious King of France garbed in one of those stinking, grease-caked, urine-stained costumes of an Indian child. What the boy king no doubt wanted was a miniature of a chief's suit, a picture of which he may have seen; or he may have heard a description which mercifully omitted all the accustomed foulness of Indian clothing.

The Jesuits knew they could not send him the authentic thing. It would never do. They must have the clothing made especially for him. At their own expense—because neither the King nor his counselors nor his mother, the Queen Regent, had thought of sending any money for the costume—they hired a Huron woman to make four complete outfits. They were soft and beautiful, embroidered with the fleur-de-lis and heavily beaded. In October, when Louis Jolliet was a month old, the suits were ready and were packed to go on the last boat, for M. de Repentigny to carry them in person and present them to the King. The Jesuits, thankful to be finished with the project, only hoped he would be pleased.

It was no wonder the Québec colony languished. This boy king had scant knowledge of it, and Cardinal Mazarin, who had been groomed by Richelieu as Minister of War as well as of spiritual affairs, evidently cared little. As long as the beaver furs came in ships of the One Hundred Associates, and as long as the Queen Regent followed in all things that Mazarin, whom she adored, should dictate, the minister was satisfied. As for the King, instead of studying about the conditions in America, and concerning himself with the Indians who were bent on wiping out all of French-Canada, the boy was only interested in masquerading himself as an Indian in the unlikely habitat of the royal palace. But he was only a boy, New France defended loyally. He could not know how bad things were. It was up to his ministers to know, however, and they were doing nothing.

The palace in France was a world away from the rock of Québec and from the little boy named Louis Jolliet who, from his earliest years knew firsthand about Indians and listened to tales brought in from the forest. The sufferings of the Jesuits out in the Huron and Iroquois missions of the wilderness were intensely real. For, when he was born, the Iroquois were even then raiding the St. Lawrence valley, and no home, in town or out, was safe from their horror. They had formerly come in great bands to the river to trade their furs, but now they were scattering into the wilderness as a perpetual menace to any peaceable Indian or white man who got in their way. Yet, in spite of the mounting and ever-present danger, the Jesuit missionaries went calmly out to try to convert these savages to Christianity.

In 1643, the Iroquois had captured the Jesuit Father Isaac Jogues. He managed to send word to Montréal to beware, that the Iroquois were out for blood and no place on the river was safe; but that he, so long as God willed, would continue to dwell a captive among them, forgiving and patient and enduring. For, he said, to the French, Hurons, and Algonquins taken with him he was their only consolation, their one link with God; he had baptized sixty of the Indians, and he would remain there to do what he could.

And he did remain. He was later rescued, but he went back again, and again he was carried prisoner among Iroquois tribes. This selfless zeal of the French missionaries often seemed to exceed sense or caution. In spite of evidently accomplishing nothing if they died at the hands of those whom they attempted to convert, they dared torture and death and went back for more.

None of them had any illusions about what happened when one was taken by the Iroquois. They were beasts. They were torturers. They were, worst of all, cannibals. One might, for the glory of God, contemplate torture and death at the hands of savages, but to be torn apart and eaten afterward was an insupportably offensive thought. Isaac Jogues knew this. And he was tortured with some of the most exquisite Iroquois refinements of pain—his fingernails torn out, the small bones in his fingers ground and crushed, the end of his thumb cut off, his body stripped naked as he was made to run a gantlet of thorny branches and clubs until he was nearly dead. Yet, with his fingers an agony, he could manage to write, to tell in careful, unimpassioned detail of his experiences and eventually send his report to his superior in Québec.

Yet it was not so much his own physical torment which caused him grief. In that astonishing abnegation, the total relinquishing of the mortal and the blossoming of the soul, he was only grieved because the Hurons whom he had baptized and who had started on the way to becoming good Christians had been so cruelly slain by the Iroquois.

So there we were [Father Jogues wrote with his poor crippled fingers], on the way to be led into a country truly foreign. It is true that, during the thirteen days that we spent on that journey, I suffered in the body torments almost unendurable, and in the soul mortal anguish; hunger; the fiercely burning heat, the threat and hatred of those Leopards, the pain of our wounds,—which, for not being dressed, became putrid even to the extent of breeding worms,—caused us, in truth, much distress. But all these things seemed light to me in comparison with an inward sadness which I felt at the sight of our earliest and most ardent Christians of the Hurons. I had thought that they were to be the pillars of the rising church, and I saw them become the victims of death. The ways closed for a long time to the salvation of so many people made me die every hour in the depth of my soul.

And so gentle Father Jogues suffered. He never knew what abuse or indignity would be put upon him next, or when some new form of torture would be committed upon his frail and long-suffering body, or when he would at last be released by death. As his biographer, Father Vimont, wrote: "A lesser courage had died a hundred times from apprehension. It is easier to die all at once than to die a hundred times."

Then at last it happened. Father Jogues had been killed, his head cut off and set on palings outside the lodges of the Iroquois, his body thrown into the river.

Louis Jolliet was two years old when the news came to Québec and his family out in Beauport learned of it. Knowledge of the atrocity hit Québec hard. People were inured to hardship and accustomed to violence and terror. They lived too close to the Indian country, were too often hit by a raid on the outskirts, ever to consider the Indians casually, but, like people living in the shadow of a volcano which may destroy them all in a night, they counted on providence and the goodness of God to protect them.

They themselves were often sinful. They were only human and they humbly accepted the fact. That was what the priests were for, to pray for them, to hear their confessions, to wash away the sins of Saturday night on Sunday morning, and to help them to be as pure as possible for another week. But for one of the anointed, for good Father Jogues, one of the most blessed, a true saint, to have perished so foully at the hands of the savages was a blow to the pit of every man's stomach. If the good should die so shamefully, then what might not happen to the wicked?

The Jolliets talked in worried horror about it over supper; and little Louis, who was old enough to sit at table and spoon soup into his mouth without getting too much down his blouse, listened with his big eyes wide and thoughtful and frightened. His brother Adrien listened—Adrien was old enough to know what it all meant. His sister Marie began to weep into her soup and had to be excused to wipe her eyes and blow her nose. The new baby, Zacharie, was oblivious to terror or tragedy or to the menace of the Iroquois.

Robert Giffard, Louis Maheu, and some of the other neighbors came in. The men who gathered in the warm kitchen that autumn night in 1647 talked of this thing that had hap-

pened. They were men who smelled of beaver fur and
salmon and codfish, men who knew the measure of the
wilderness. But no man could help but fear the Iroquois,
who were without conscience and without mercy. The men
who gathered in the Jolliet kitchen, as well as the people of
Québec who were also discussing it that worried night, felt
helpless and futile to combat this menace. If the king would
only see fit to send some soldiers!

Next, the Iroquois killed brawny Father Jean de Bréboeuf
and Father Gabriel L'Alemant in the country of the Hurons.
Eight Jesuits eventually were martyred.

It was in 1649—Louis Jolliet was then just past four—that
two small chests made of birch bark were brought reverently
to Québec—down the rivers, out of the Huron country, to
the great gray rock brooding in the November light that lay
pale blue and dreaming over the far-off Laurentians and the
river. The two small chests containing the bones of the martyrs, Father Bréboeuf and Father L'Alemant, had been
brought lovingly for interment in a decent Christian location.

The bones lay in honor and veneration on the altar of the
Jesuit chapel, where Marie d'Abancourt and her children
went to see them and to pray.

And so it went, one after another; the Jesuits were dying
at the hand of the people of the forest whom they had hoped
to save. And the little boy, listening and thinking about it,
perhaps even then began to form a deep desire to try to follow in the revered footsteps of these saints.

Louis was growing tall and strong. His father, however, sometimes felt discouraged at how little the child
seemed to be interested in learning a craft. Neither did the
boy seem interested in the beaver trade which was the
principal business along the river, from Tadoussac to Montréal.

Adrien, unlike his brother, had for some time been helping his uncles to prepare the pelts brought in when the Indian canoes came down the river each summer. Adrien had a feeling for the wilderness and all that came out of it. He talked of when he would be old enough to go out with the fur men, to hunt out the wonders of the far western wilderness, to see unknown rivers that lay out there. Sometimes the two boys made plans of going out to the wilderness together, and vowed they would take Zacharie, the youngest, when he should be old enough. But aside from these boyish plans and dreams, Louis seemed only to be interested in music and in drawing pictures and crude charts which he called maps.

To Jean Jolliet, a son who was interested in music and art was a discouragement, even though the child was far too young to have made up his mind about anything. Art was good; Jean approved of it. Music was good, too. There were none who enjoyed it more, especially a lively violin playing of an evening for songs and dancing. But he needed his sons to grow up to support him when he was unable to do so himself. He wanted them to become prosperous traders and merchants, or perhaps fishermen, or trappers, or sailors, all honorable professions. Music and art wouldn't earn a man a living in the wilderness of this forsaken country. But Louis perversely was happiest with these.

Jean Jolliet did not have time to worry for very long about what his sons would or would not do. In the long winter of 1651, when faulty diet and hardship brought on many illnesses, Jean was laid low by a fever in his lungs. High temperatures and congested lungs could not be combatted, and in spite of the prayers and the ministrations of his wife and Dr. Giffard, Jean grew weaker. The priest was sent for over the thawing trails of April, and arrived in time to administer the last rites. Then Jean Jolliet died.

The children went about in a silent, stunned manner. It was hard for them to understand that their hearty, joking, hard-working father was gone away forever. Marie, too, for a time was full of grief.

But in a land in which women were scarce and men needed women as much as the latter needed the protection of the men, no female, unless she insisted upon remaining single, stayed long unmarried. Marie d'Abancourt Jolliet, a short time after Jean's death, married Godefroid Guillot. And the family moved to Québec.

Godefroid Guillot was a fairly prosperous trader who had a good stone house in the lower town. There was enough money to send the three boys to the Jesuits for their classical education and young Marie to the Ursulines to learn to read and write, embroider and sew.

It was with the Jesuits that Louis Jolliet discovered the world of books. In 1655, when he was ten, he began studying in earnest. At the seminary he was handy to all the books he wanted, to musical instruments, to paper and drawing materials, and to men who did not consider the classical arts and pursuits wasteful and of no value. His ability in drawing grew with encouragement and practice. He delighted in making maps, as well as careful and intricate drawings of church symbols, of scenes in the street, of ships in the harbor, of whatever he could see around him.

When he was thirteen, Louis made a map of the St. Lawrence River. It included everything he had seen or heard about, though his own experiences on the river were really very limited. He had even put in a very faulty Anticosti Island out in the Gulf of St. Lawrence. He knew his map was not really accurate, he explained shyly to the priest who examined it in the light coming through the leaded window. Some day he would go along the entire river, the boy went on, embarrassed by the teacher's silence as he examined the map; he would draw the river so accurately that pilots could use it.

The priest smiled at the earnest boy and assured him that it was indeed an excellent map, but that there was something he should always remember. He must be honest; if there was no integrity in his maps, no one would trust them. Therefore, he should wait to see each place himself, in its relation to the surrounding places, before he drew it on his map. Then he would know it was correct, and his own assurance would assure those who needed to put their lives in the safety of what he had set down. The boy listened, and he never forgot . . . to see things himself, to set down only what he saw.

The Jesuits kept the map. He may have wished to have it back, but the priests must have seen something in it which was more than a thirteen-year-old boy's scribbling. They may have felt that they were seeing the seeds of something good and great, as many a teacher has seen with an inner excitement. In the archives of the Jesuit Seminary they laid away the boy's map of the St. Lawrence.

When school was out in summer, Louis went to Trois Rivières with Adrien to help their stepfather and uncles at the fur warehouse. Between times, the two liked to go out exploring up the St. Maurice River. They would have enjoyed doing some trapping so they could sell their pelts and make a little money, but pelts were not good in summer and Adrien had learned from experience that the fussy fur men scorned summer skins which he had had the temerity to offer. They were hardly worth the effort in summer; and in winter the boys were busy in school.

The two had fun along the river, fishing sometimes and watching animals that came down to drink when the two were quiet on the banks. They talked a great deal and planned how, when they were both old enough, they would go out together to the western wilderness at last and find lands no one had ever seen before.

The two had been told sternly never to go very far away from Trois Rivières, and never for one of them to go out alone to the forest. But on a warm day in June, when Louis was taking an examination in Québec, Adrien, who at nearly eighteen felt as dependable as a man, went out alone along the St. Maurice. Although he had no intention of doing so, he somehow wandered farther and farther, following a trail which he and Louis had never seen before. He decided to find out more about it. When Louis was back he could show it to him, and they could continue a little farther.

The trail was only a deer path, he thought, and, after the manner of deer paths, it started at the river and went in a fairly direct manner into the thickets of balsam firs, then began to ramble, as a deer path so often does. It suddenly ended indecisively in a thicket of firs, in a sort of "room" enclosed by the tall, fragrant, dark-green trees, with a summer-crisped bed of gray reindeer moss and wintergreen carpeting it. Here the deer had evidently lain down to rest and nibble moss and leaves.

When he turned to retrace his steps, Adrien could not tell where the path was. The branches of the firs had closed in behind him and there was no indication of any path at all. He pushed through the trees in several places, but saw no sign of a trail. Finally he tried again and saw what he thought was the route by which he had come. But instead of leading him back to the river it seemed to be taking an unreasonably long way around to get him there. It began to mount a ridge, and then he knew he was lost.

Adrien had spent too much time in the woods during his life to feel very much alarmed at this. The sun was still high and it would be no trick at all to orient himself, find the

stony rapids of the St. Maurice, and follow its route directly
back to Trois Rivières.

While he scanned trees and sky, the Indians were upon
him before he had any inkling of their presence. He was
furious with himself at his stupidity. He had prided himself
on his woods knowledge, but he had forgotten to be wary.
They were Iroquois. Hurons he could have spoken with; he
knew a few words of their tongue, but not Iroquois. But the
Indians were in no mood to listen to him. Though he pro-
tested and held back, they slapped him hard and forced him
to go ahead. Stumbling over the smooth shield-rock and
slippery bearberry bushes, he had to go whether he wanted
to or not.

Adrien Jolliet did not come home that night. There was
no trace of the boy when his stepfather and uncles went
out to search for him. On June 13, 1658, Adrien had simply
vanished from the eyes of his world.

When Louis came next day, his examination passed with
honors, he could not believe what they told him. The men
had gone out again on a longer hunt, but few felt they would
have any luck. If the boy had been merely lost or hurt, he
would have heard them shouting. If the Indians had taken
him, he would already be far away. But they hunted anyway. There was nothing else to do, and they couldn't face
the misery in Marie Jolliet Guillot's anguished face.

Marie paced and wrung her hands. She prayed before the
family shrine, prayed at the cathedral, promising any sort
of penitence if only her first-born should be returned to her
in safety. Louis was ready to start off on his own to hunt
for his brother, but his mother screamed and restrained him,
crying that she had lost one son and could not bear to lose
another.

But Louis was not frightened for his brother; not yet. He
knew how strong and reliant Adrien was in the woods, too

wise to be vanquished by a forest. Adrien, who knew the
ways of the beavers in their lodges, the secret paths of the
deer and elk, the trails where the best blueberries grew; who
could take the bark from birch trees and make a canoe almost as expertly as an Indian. Louis knew that Adrien was
levelheaded and didn't take chances. He would not be afraid
of the wilderness or of the Indians, either. But when Louis
thought of the Indians, he was not so confident.

The men came back without any success. Some of them
searched on the second day, but there was no sign of the
boy. The days went by and Marie Guillot went about in a
preoccupied state. She cried easily and spent much time before the figure of the Blessed Virgin, or went to the church
to pray and light a candle. Louis prayed, too, but he had not
given up hope of finding Adrien alive as his mother had.
Now she prayed for the soul of one she felt was irretrievably
lost, slain somewhere by the savages, as Father Jogues and
the other martyrs had been.

The days and weeks went by, and two months had passed
with no sign of the boy, when someone outside the warehouse looked up to see a tall, elderly Indian walking rapidly
with a lean, brown-skinned young man along the trail beside the St. Maurice. The fur man gave a surprised shout
which brought out the others.

It was indeed Adrien, brown and healthy, not at all unhappy, and smelling like an Indian. With him was Chief
Garakontie, a Christianized Iroquois of impeccable character
and esteem among the French.

Garakontie, in abject embarrassment and apology, tried
to explain what had happened. He had labored very hard
and long to keep the peace between the French and his own
hotheaded and vindictive people who were continually in-
cited by the English to make raids on the French, and were

well paid for doing it. After all his efforts, then, to come
upon a village up in the back country above Trois Rivières,
in the wilderness along the rapids of the St. Maurice and
near the edge of the mountains, and find a French boy there
—it had shocked the old chief. He had vigorously and in-
dignantly harangued the men of the village on the evils of
their ways, promising them that their sins would surely
cause their downfall and the ruin of all their people. To have
made off with a French boy—it was unbelievable, after all
his preaching and his threats!

In great concern and worry, he had hurriedly taken Adrien
Jolliet back to his people at Trois Rivières.

Adrien was glad enough to be home. He had missed Louis
and his mother and the fur men at the warehouse, too, but he
had not really suffered at the hands of the Iroquois, and
he had learned a great deal. During his summer of captivity
he had grown proficient in their tongue. He had made many
friends among his captors. His outgoing nature and his will-
ingness to learn Indian ways had pleased the surly Iroquois
who grudgingly came to admire the boy. They would have
kept him there if they could have done so without angering
the powerful Garakontie.

By the time Adrien came back to his people, he could
speak Iroquois fluently—and a Frenchman with this ability
possessed an enviable talent. Few had a chance to live long
enough, once they were captured by the Iroquois, to learn
anything, much less the nuances of this complicated language.

The relief he felt at his brother's rescue sent Louis Jolliet
that fall into his studies with an even greater enthusiasm.
When he completed his classical course, he was still far from
ready to finish his education and go to work with Adrien at
the warehouse. Besides, more and more, the priesthood was

calling to him. Toward this end he now studied with intensity and fervor.

In 1662 he received minor orders in the sodality chapel of the Jesuits, from the hand of his friend, Monseigneur François de Montmorency-Laval.

As an energetic cleric, Laval at thirty-six years of age had come to Québec in 1659. Someone must reorganize the failing educational system and bring order out of the chaos attending the neglected church and its missions, and Laval was the man to do it. Ascetic and benevolent, he was revered by all who knew him. He was devoted to the welfare of Québec, to the education of its young, to the glory of music, and to a complete disregard for personal comfort. Though once very rich, he had given up all his wealth when he left France. He slept willingly with vermin in his hard, straw-tick bed and wore unwashed linen for months on end, for the purity of his soul. It might have been said at times that, on close acquaintance, the good prelate sometimes bore a strong scent when one was to windward, but the beauty of dedication shining on his good face more than offset one's delicacy of nostril.

There was a fire in Louis Jolliet which attracted the fire in Bishop Laval. Both of them loved Canada and the river, and they both loved God and the beauty of music. Whenever he could, Laval helped Louis Jolliet, and the strong, intent young man grew deeply devoted to the thoughtful, experienced prelate. To emulate him, to become a good priest and to serve the people of the wilderness, was all that Louis now wished.

Meanwhile, as he studied, music engrossed him. He and Germain Morin were the performing musicians of the seminary. Amador Martin composed plainsongs and chants. Louis learned to play the harpsichord, the flute, and the trumpet, so that he could perform for masses. There was a small, wheezing organ in the chapel and a somewhat better one in the cathedral upon which Louis also performed, but Bishop Laval, soon after he came, felt that Québec should have a really fine instrument for the new stone cathedral. Laval believed that music had a large and important place in the worship of God.

Almost from their very beginning, the churches in Canada had had music. They might have had little else—no seats at first, few candles, and there might be Indians lurking in the bushes—but they still had music. Violins, violas, cellos, trumpets, and flutes came with the first religious orders to this harsh wilderness, and they were played for services. Each church organized a boys' choir as soon as possible, and there were always choirs of nuns and seminarists in Québec.

What they had, however, Laval insisted, was good enough for a beginning, and very commendable, too, but he was obsessed with the need for greater heights. When he went to France on church business in 1662, he purchased a large pipe organ and brought it back, together with men to build, install, and tune it.

Installation, however, was slow and difficult. Local artisans had to be taught how to do the work. Meanwhile, an energetic priest studied the mechanism piece by piece as it was being assembled, all the ranks of pipes both great and small, the reeds and stops and keyboards and pedals—all—so that he could build one for himself later on. From this seed sprang many lesser organs for the scattered churches of French Canada.

The new organ did not find its voice until Christmas Eve, 1664. Then, as the people gathered for midnight Mass in the hushed candlelight of the cathedral, the voice of the organ began at last, at first low and small, as if at a distance, thoughtfully, then rising in a splendid volume to soar into

the clerestory, to swell and fade beyond the windows into
the driving snow of midnight. The nuns and seminarists sang,
and the children's choir performed angelically enough even
to satisfy Bishop Laval. The congregation knelt, souls and
hearts uplifted on a glory of majestic music as it had never
been heard in America before.

There is no record of who played those Christmas hymns
and the Mass on the great organ, but since Louis Jolliet was
the only accomplished organist in Québec at that time, it
was surely he, his heart exulting in the power of music, who
played the midnight Mass when the great organ first found
its voice.

Adrien and his mother, her husband, young Marie and her
husband, and Zacharie, and no doubt all the kinfolk, were
there to hear Louis perform. It was a time of tremendous
pride for the whole family to see one of them rising to such
heights of glory. But Adrien, listening to the swelling emotion in the music, realized with an inner sadness that Louis
would never come with him to explore the wilderness. The
church and the music had him in their exacting and splendid
thralldom.

4

~~~~~~

WORD OF A RIVER

ENGROSSED AS HE WAS in the church and its music, Louis
Jolliet had not been very much affected by what had been
happening in the years between 1661 and 1667. To Canada
and to Québec, however, the events were vital and stirring.

In France, the boy who in 1645 had demanded Red Indian
garments from the strange wilderness of New France, had
grown to a manhood dominated largely by cardinal, ministers, and mother. When he was twenty-five, Louis XIV
suddenly decided that he was ready to make his own de-
cisions and dominate his kingdom. He was finished with
depending upon others. He wanted no more of the bungling
which had gone on unchecked during his youth. Now he
would be king in more than name.

It was the year 1661, and Cardinal Mazarin was dead. To
the young king it seemed that at that moment a great weight
had been removed from his neck, and from his country as
well. Mazarin, the disciple of the implacable Richelieu, had
carried on what that cardinal-minister had begun earlier in
the century, had ruled the Queen, dominated trade and war,
had neglected the Canadian colony. But now Mazarin was
gone.

Changes set in almost at once. In 1663, the King dissolved
the ineffectual Company of One Hundred Associates. Its

members had failed to keep their contract in financing the colonization of New France in return for the benefits of trade, and recently had sent only scant profits back to the King. It was time that something be done to put Canada on its feet or it would be destroyed by attrition.

To remedy the desperate situation, New France was declared a crown land directly under the King and the colonial minister, Colbert. Able men were assigned to take over the government, with their power divided so that no one man should be wholly responsible for the administration, the successes, or the mistakes of the colony.

The new lieutenant-general was Alexandre de Prouville, the Marquis de Tracy. Daniel de Rémy, the Sieur de Courcelles, was made governor, while, as intendant or assistant to him, capable Jean Talon was put in charge of all the details of government. As superintendant of New France, it was his often thankless and endless job to carry out the orders of his superiors and see that laws were made and obeyed, that the land was defended against English and Iroquois, that all problems were taken care of through him, and the land developed at last.

Talon was a vigorous man of tact and diplomacy. He could at once cajole the nobles and order the common man, yet offend neither; and he had a special way with Indians. He had complete concern for the welfare of Canada. That was why he was there. After so many years of neglect, of being left to their own poorly supplied devices, the people of Canada found this devotion a strange and heart-warming experience. Even more impressive were the twelve companies of soldiers, all smartly uniformed and armed, from the Carignan-Salières regiment, and the inspiring job they did in subduing the Indians and obtaining a treaty of peace.

Talon was determined to improve living conditions and the economic situation in Québec. Many of the people, however, had grown indolent and they certainly had no special wish to be improved or, worse yet, to be put to work. For years it had been considered a good deal easier and far more profitable for a man to go off into the forest as a *coureur des bois,* and to come back eventually with a splendid supply of beaver pelts to be sold at the warehouses, than to work hard at clearing land, uprooting stumps and rocks, and planting crops. Garden patches provided a few vegetables. There were cows, when the Indians didn't steal them. There were always fish in the river or a deer up in the woods. Why work so hard?

Jean Talon decided with vigor to change this deplorable state of Gallic indolence. Canada would never become strong or of any use to France or to itself by such laziness and do-nothingness. He organized the colonists who had built houses between Québec and Montréal and arranged them in small towns. He divided the surrounding lands into long narrow strip farms, the houses and barns facing the river and the land stretching far back. He offered medals of distinction for the best results from uses of the soil.

But it was still too much work for the rewards. What was a medal and a pat on the shoulder from Monsieur the Intendant for the back-breaking work a man must endure to bring forth anything from a field, even after he had taken off the trees and removed the endless and execrable stones? There were an expressive shrug and an outward wave of the hands that said more than words. Beaver fur—ah, now that was the thing. Easy work left more time for pleasure.

To combat the latter inclination, the intendant promptly put a restriction on the fur trade. A man now had to have a permit and a license to go out to the forest, and these were suddenly very hard to get. Only twenty-five in a year were to be given. There was a sudden dearth of beaver in the warehouses, hardly any fox or otter, moose or mink. The price of pelts rose. Men raged. Here was the chance to get rich, and they weren't permitted to secure the animals that would do it.

Some defied the law. They were the pugnacious *coureurs des bois* who went back to the wilderness, stayed for a year or two, and suddenly reappeared long enough to dispose of a load of pelts, spend money on brandy and presents for the women, and then vanish again before the authorities could apprehend them. The *coureurs des bois* had become outlaws from the king's orders. Soon there was a ruling that they were to be apprehended, fined or imprisoned, or both. That is, if they could be caught. But the wilderness was wide and the forest deep; any bushranger who was skilled enough to exist in the far places of the north had sense enough to elude the law, and he did it with an insolence and ease which was infuriating to those in authority.

But not all Québec men were insubordinate or lazy. Many earnest settlers began to work the land. From long narrow fields which still exist along the St. Lawrence, fenced with rocks or sprawling pine roots, agriculture, with pain and often with discouragement but with growing success, slowly began to develop around Québec. With it came better living conditions, better food, better courage, and more self-respect.

Talon was disturbed by the brandy trade, so he had a brewery built in Québec to regulate the supply of beer and ale; he put restrictions on the sale of liquor, especially to Indians. Not only the development of home resources filled Talon's tremendous program: he needed to know more about the western wilderness and to develop its resources, too. He sent men out to hunt for mines along the Great Lakes. In the other direction, to the east, he encouraged the fishing for cod and salmon, and built up the business of seal hunting, for seal oil was immensely valuable and could become a profitable export.

As Talon labored, his people were beginning at last to realize something of what Québec and Canada could be. Then in 1667 Father Claude Allouez came back from his La Pointe mission on Chequamegon Bay at the far western end of Lake Superior, the church's most remote point, to ask for an assistant in his labors in that great unknown country.

With him he brought two things for the intendant— word of an unknown great river which the Indians called "Messipi," and a handful of fine specimens of copper ore.

Both items fascinated Talon. The river might indeed be that still-sought key to the northern mystery and the route to the Great South Sea which he and France had never quite ceased to hope one day to locate, but the copper was of more real and immediate interest. One of the orders which the King had given Talon was to seek out copper mines and find out how to exploit them and bring their wealth to Québec and thence to France.

The Jesuits' house was home to all the Jesuits in Canada, their haven when they came back from the mission field, the loving welcome of their black-clad brothers a glorious spiritual refreshment after years of harshness and rebuffs among the Indians. To Father Allouez, his shabby gown, showing the effects of laborious travel through wilderness, and his face lined with fatigue, the open door of the Jesuits' house and the welcome within gave him new life.

Louis Jolliet was among those who greeted the returned priest and saw that he was made comfortable. Louis with deep interest then heard what Allouez told about the great wilderness of the western lake country, of the copper mine, and of the unknown river. Once again, flooding back into his consciousness, came the old dreams which he and Adrien had had of going to the west to explore.

5

~~~~~~~~

THE DECISION

PERHAPS IT WAS ALL SETTLED in his mind long before Father
Allouez came back from the western wilderness. Perhaps the
coming of the missionary only crystallized what he had by
then known he must do; or, it may have had nothing at all
to do with it. No one knows.

But Louis Jolliet went one day to see Bishop Laval. He
told him that he could no longer remain in the service of
God. He must leave the seminary.

Louis was deeply troubled. Something had gone wrong.
Somewhere along the way he had lost something which had
been part of himself: faith, perhaps, or knowledge that he
was intended to be of the church, sublimating self in service
to God. He could not, however, continue in the way he was
going, could not pursue his theological studies to the point
of conviction and supreme dedication which he would need
in order to remain a priest for the rest of his life.

Uneasy, regretful, disturbed by his own inner turmoil, disgusted by such vacillation in a spirit which he had believed
to be firm in its convictions, he talked to his friend the
bishop. One could always tell his troubles to the good Bishop
of Petraea, who would lean down and lay his thin hand on
the head of penitent or sinner, on the worried and the unsure, and give absolution and the confidence to go on.

Louis Jolliet knew it would somehow be all right if Laval released him from his vows—if the bishop understood that it was not for loving God the less but because . . . because of something he could not explain. He only knew he could not continue his studies. The life outside and the call of the wilderness were as the singing of sirens whose voices outbid the quieter voices within the seminary walls.

Unlike the priests who were sent afield and who were required to return their detailed accounts back to the superior, and who thus could insert their personalities and their fears and inner thoughts into these reports, Louis never set down the reasons why he left the seminary and went out into a world in which he never, really, had had any experience in making his way. He was twenty-two and a man who was now about to be on his own, and he didn't even own a suit of clothes, not even the long gown of the Jesuit in which he knelt before the bishop in the untidy office he maintained.

He knew his mother would help if she could, but she had little money of her own. Marie Jolliet had married a third time, after Godefroid Guillot drowned in the St. Lawrence. Louis could imagine the comments which her newest husband, M. Prévost, would make concerning his ne'er-do-well stepson.

But there was always Adrien, who had many a time asked Louis to come into the fur business with him. Adrien, married three years before to pretty Jeanne Dodier, was now established at Cap-de-la-Madeleine, father of a son. He could use Louis in the warehouse, but he certainly would not have much cash to lend him for a start elsewhere.

But before he would get into any business here, something else intervened. One of the mysteries of his life is not only that Louis Jolliet decided to leave the seminary, but that he went at once to France. No one really knows what he did there, though many conjectures have been made.

His going may have been at Laval's suggestion, for it was the bishop who provided him the money for clothes, for his passage, and for all his expenses while in France. He may indeed have studied there briefly, as has been suggested, with the chief mapmaker of France, M. Franquelin. But this, too, is not known with any certainty or proof. The times were not such that a young man of no means and no prospects, and with no relatives abroad, would suddenly go to France on a pleasure trip. There must have been a reason.

He borrowed 587 livres from Bishop Laval and, in a new suit of clothes, hat, shoes, and with a box containing his extra garments, he boarded a ship in the harbor where for so many years he had watched ships come and go. When it finally set off with Louis Jolliet aboard, the sails bellying out in the river wind, he must have felt a rising surge of excitement.

As the vessel moved in calm and stately departure down the river toward the sea, he could discover, as if he were looking at a giant-sized map of his own making, how the great cleft of the continent filled by the river widened beyond the Île d'Orléans, until the shores with their colorful autumn trees were far and hazy on either side. He saw bays and rivers which he had never seen before, passed the Saguenay where a troop of white whales leaped and blew in dark water, and knew that someday he must take a canoe up that great split where the Saguenay emerged, and find out whence it came.

The ship passed the curve of the Gaspé and he saw it glide into the mists of the Gulf of St. Lawrence. The ship was passing through a sealike embayment which surely must be the ocean itself. There were the salt smell and the crying of seabirds, and the great spray-tossing dives of the black and white gannets.

But he had not yet passed the great shiplike bulk of Anticosti Island, lying athwart the Gulf of St. Lawrence. He had
put that island on the map he made when he was thirteen,
and had wondered then what it really looked like. Now he
peered through the growing fog wraiths to see a great wild
and rocky island covered with forest, humping over what
must be cliffs in the middle. The trees near shore were
weather-beaten and gnarled on the windward side where
storms from the Atlantic wracked them year by year. There
were rocky beaches where every tide rolled the polished
pebbles with a grating rattle. There were headlands, and
there were rivers flowing over flats into the sea, and open
places now and again where there might have been house or
fort if any people had settled there. No one lived on grim,
wild Anticosti.

And then they were safely past the island and its reefs,
rounding the dim, distant point and heading into a fog
which grew thicker until the ship moved only slowly, creep-
ing, drifting in no wind. They slid through the Cabot Straits
between Newfoundland and Cape Breton, and, as the ship
bore him away from the sight and sound of land, he was on
the fog-thickened open sea at last. He knew with finality
that he had left Canada behind him.

To most of the adults in Canada, the mother country was
still France, but to him and to his generation there was not
the blood-pull to any native land except America, back there
with its spruce forests and its rivers. Suddenly, while gannets
and petrels scaled past in the fog, Louis Jolliet for the first
time in his life felt a twinge of homesickness.

The ship crossed the Atlantic in about two and a half long
and tedious, storm-tossed months and entered the Bay of
Biscay. The vessel landed at La Rochelle on the west coast
of France on a biting winter day when the sailors' fingers
were half frozen and the cordage was bitter with ice and salt

rime. When he went ashore it was with a curious feeling of being in a foreign land, in spite of the fact that only his native tongue was spoken. It was a foreign land, an old land soaked in blood and desperation and hardship, in the tyranny of kings and the ancient wars of Europe.

It didn't smell like America. There was a mustiness in the winter air, a stink of garbage in the streets, of slops thrown from windows and lying fetid and frozen in the gutters. There was an ancientness about the port city which he would find in Paris, too, and wherever he went, except in the open country.

France was old. It looked old and smelled decayed, and he knew he would not be there too long before the lure of the New World and its freshness and excitement would take him quickly away. He would fulfill what Bishop Laval wished, perhaps might consult M. Franquelin and learn some of the additional points in hydrography which his teachers in Québec had been unable to teach him. But it would not be long before he would take a ship home, perhaps early the next summer when vessels again were heading west to New France. Canada was his country and his destiny, not this, the homeland of his parents.

Still, it must have been an exciting experience for the young man who had never been away from home before to see the life of Paris, to feel caught up in the atmosphere which bred court life and the undercurrents of history which were always in the making behind Paris shutters and in the ballrooms and elaborate chambers of the King. Not that he took part in any of these. The priesthood and the simple life of a wheelwright's son in Canada had not fitted him to enter into social or court life, even if he had had the opportunity.

But to meet with M. Franquelin, the great cartographer, was an honor and a delight. With his keen and eager mind, Louis learned a great deal in a short time under this master of the art of translating land and waters and shores to the language of lines on a sheet of paper.

Louis also visited a friend of Bishop Laval, whom the bishop had specifically requested him to see and to whom he sent an introductory letter. Charles de Lauzon-Charny was the youngest son of the fourth governor-general of Canada, and had come back to France at his father's death to manage the estate. It was exceedingly good to be invited to M. de Charny's fine house, to stay to dinner and a long evening of talk, because Monsieur knew Canada and it was comforting for one away for the first time to be able to speak of things about which they both knew. They could laugh over the same jokes about the governor, could praise or castigate with praiseworthy thoroughness, and then laugh again over the wine.

Evenings at the de Charny chateau were exhilarating, and when it was time to leave Louis went out into the dark, snowy streets of Paris and found his way to the house of the parish priest of St. Josse, Father Poitevin, where he had his modest lodging.

Compared with Québec winters, this one seemed short and not at all severe. When he woke one morning and found that springtime was bursting the almond trees into fragrant bloom, he could hardly believe that the time could have come so soon. The air was delirious with life and excitement, and he knew he must go home. He couldn't stand it any longer. Yet, as he lay there breathing the perfume of the almond trees and listening to a hoopoe crying, he knew it would be a senseless thing to run back home on the very first ship that would take him to Canada. After all, the bishop had lent him a great deal of money to do this thing, and he would be a thankless and witless fool to leave before he had at least finished his work with M. Franquelin. He would wait. But the hoopoe's calling and the almond flowers were hard to reconcile. He kept thinking of wild plum blossoms along the St. Maurice, and the cries of geese going north to the Mistassini country, and the poignant caroling of the first thrush come back to his mother's garden. The longing for home was almost too much to bear.

He stayed until August, 1668. Then, finished with Paris, with La Rochelle, with all of France, Louis Jolliet sailed for Canada.

He knew he was nearing America even before the ship came in sight of land, long before he saw the Madeleines or the chill bulk of the Newfoundland coast, or Anticosti lying athwart the bay. There was the faint, rich smell of ripened maple leaves as it had been when he left the year before, and in his mind's eye he could again see the great blaze of the forests along the river flaring their autumn colors to the crisp and sparkling air of Canada, color muted by the blue haze along the river and over the distant bulk of the Laurentians and the Shickshocks.

In his imagination he could hear the sound of the snow geese like bells high in the deep blue of an autumn sky, could remember how the big birds fluttered like bits of white paper, coming down suddenly on the river or in the marshes.

It was hardly a surprise when, as the ship moved into the river, the flocks of white geese began passing over the ship. When he saw them, he knew he was almost home. The gannets again were plummeting from the heights and diving deep for fish. Gaunt, black shags sat on rocks along the shores, and rotund seals tumbled and slid from rocks as the vessel went slowly past.

As the shores began to close in, as the cleft narrowed to become the river proper, he could almost have wept, filled as he was with the Gallic sentiment of homecoming. This

was his country, and he must never leave it again. The Old
World was covered with the ugly mold of the past. America
was new and fresh and it held both hope and challenge, and
it smelled so good!

None of his family met the ship. None of them had known
when he was coming. He sprinted up the streets to his
mother's house and engulfed her in a great hug, while she
kissed him and wept on his neck, and fondled him with the
emotion of a mother long deprived of a beloved child. Her
husband, M. Prévost, greeted Louis with cordiality, and
Zacharie, who was home after a summer at the warehouse
at Sault Ste Marie with Adrien, came bursting in with all the
aliveness of the forest and waters about him. He gripped
Louis by the arms and danced about with him in a joy which
removed from him all the loneliness of Paris and the sea.
He was home! He could hardly wait to see Adrien and tell
him that he would go with him in the spring when he went
to the Sault. Family ties were close. Now the three Jolliet
brothers would at last be allied with a common love and
purpose in the family business.

To make certain that he had his trade goods ready,
Louis, soon after his return, borrowed 450 livres from the
indulgent Bishop Laval, who was so happy to see him that he
would have given him almost anything he asked. On October
9, 1668, Louis Jolliet bought from his friend and kinsman,
Charles Aubert de La Chesnaye, twelve ells of cloth, a hat
and two pairs of shoes, two guns and two pistols—these for
his own use. Then, on Adrien's advice, he purchased trade
goods for the Indians: six packages of wampum, twenty-
four hatchets, a gross of small bells, twelve ells of coarse
cloth, ten ells of canvas, and forty ounces of tobacco.

With some inner worry and a belated questioning of his
wisdom in getting so deeply in debt, Louis hoped the bishop

would not mind waiting to be repaid until there were some profits from the trading venture. The bishop insisted that he was in no hurry to be repaid. Let Louis get himself settled in the business and permit a little money to accumulate as a safeguard against disaster, and only then think of repaying.

But Adrien did not like it at all. It was against his principles to owe money any longer than he could possibly help it, and he hated to see his brother disgraced by indebtedness to anyone, much less the benevolent Bishop Laval. He went to talk with the prelate.

The subject of the discussion was of course not disclosed, but it may have been less by accident than by design that the day before Louis purchased his first items from La Chesnaye, the bishop bought from the Jolliet estate a large piece of land for 2,400 livres. Half of this sum was to be paid to the widow of the deceased Jean Jolliet, and three hundred livres to each of the four children—Adrien, Louis, Marie, and Zacharie.

Marie, the mother, decided to devote part of her windfall to paying her son's debt. She directed the bishop to withhold 180 livres from the installment payments of her share.

And Adrien decided that he had no great need for extra money at the present. At Cap-de-la-Madeleine on November 9, 1668, he sent the following note to Monseigneur Laval.

I agree that my Lord the Bishop of Petraea may hand over to my brother Louis Jolliet the 300 livres due to me as my share of the price of the land which was sold to him. In testimony thereof, I have signed the present note to serve him as receipt. Done at Cap-de-la-Madeleine, November 9, 1668.

With this amount, with his own share of the sale of land, and with that relinquished by his mother, Louis could pay back almost all of the debt to Laval. The free feeling was exhilarating. So was the knowledge that when spring came, he would start out at last with Adrien for the western wilderness.

But when spring came, Louis Jolliet did not go to the west.

6

~~~~~~~~

ADRIEN

SINCE THAT FATEFUL DAY when Father Allouez had come
back from Lake Superior and showed Talon and the Jesuits
the specimens of copper, and told of the deposits of copper, the nuggets, the scatterings of ore which even shone
through the clear lake waters, the intendant had been thinking about it. There were two more things which he especially
wanted to accomplish during his tenure in Canada. He had
already done much, but there were these two other things
which nagged at him endlessly. If God willed, they should be
Talon's memorial in the New World.

He wanted, first of all, to be instrumental in finding and
opening for use the rich copper mines of the west. And he
wanted desperately to discover a way by water on which the
French could reach the Pacific Ocean.

The more immediate need, of the two, was to find the
mines. The copper specimens in the thin, weathered, paddle-
creased brown hand of Father Allouez, touched with the
gold of Québec sunshine, had been the Grail for which
Talon had sought. To follow that Grail to the ultimate mines,
and then to find the easiest way to transport the ore back to
civilization—yes, that was the thing!

Talon wrote to the foreign minister, Colbert, in Paris, and
reported the existence of a rich copper mine in the Lake

Superior country. Colbert, with characteristic reserve and with no real knowledge of America, though interested, cautioned Talon on excess enthusiasm until it was found how to transport the ore to Québec. Colbert had heard of the interminable rivers and their dangers, of the tremendous and inconceivable American wilderness. Copper ore was heavy and these savages and colonists had nothing bigger or stronger for carrying anything on the inland waters than those incredible canoes made, of all things, from the papery bark of certain trees. Heavy barges were what were needed, and ships, to bring out ore in usable quantities from the mines of the Great Lakes. Colbert had been assured, however, by men who professed to know, that neither ore ships nor ore barges were available in Canada, nor could they ever traverse the narrow rivers, the wild rapids, the portages, or the Great Lakes.

Still, it was worth investigating, Colbert wrote cautiously to Talon. If, he said, there really was copper in the west, and if it could be easily mined, it would be something well worth following up, and the King would certainly be very much pleased if it was successful.

Talon received the letter from Colbert in 1668, shortly before, irritated by constant clashes with Governor Courcelles, he thankfully departed for a leave of absence in France in November. He knew he would be back next year, his health permitting; so before he left he appointed Jean Péré to go out to Lake Superior and locate the copper mine which had been so vividly reported by Allouez, but whose existence might be only a shadow on the face of the wilderness and in the tales of the Indians and Jesuits. Jean Péré was a fur trader, and he knew that country as well as any white man did. Bolstered with a thousand livres as subsidy, he set off even before winter began. This, in itself, was a curious thing for him to do. Only the direst of emergencies ever sent any man into the wilderness in winter.

Talon may have been belatedly concerned with whether or not he would ever see Jean Péré or the thousand livres again, so as a second thought and safeguard he decided to send another man to follow and catch up with him in the spring, as well as to take out additional supplies. One of the best and most honest of men, a veteran of the woods, sincere, good, and highly thought of by Bishop Laval himself, was Adrien Jolliet.

He paid Adrien Jolliet four hundred livres for expenses, and told him that when spring came and he could travel easily, he was to go out to Lake Superior with supplies and find where Jean Péré was and see if he had, indeed, located the copper mine. There was something he may not have quite trusted in Jean Péré, and now that it was too late to recall the man, Talon could at least send someone whom he knew to be trustworthy and to report back promptly. Adrien would, at the same time, hunt for an easier water route between Lake Superior and the St. Lawrence, with a view toward transporting any ore which might materialize from the mine. Talon knew that it would be impossible to carry ore on the rapid-filled Ottawa.

Adrien Jolliet went back in haste to Cap-de-la-Madeleine to tell Jeanne and Louis of what had happened.

In his elation, Adrien had forgotten the plans which he and Louis had made for the next year. And the intendant had specified that he should go alone and report back as soon as he had located Péré or news of him. He hated to hurt his brother. After so many years of planning on going out to the wilderness together, it was a shame to have to wait still longer. Besides, with Adrien away, it was necessary for Louis to stay in charge at the warehouse. They would go out the next year.

Louis was deeply disappointed, but discipline in the seminary had instilled in him an acceptance of disappointment. Adrien must obey the intendant's orders. Louis set his jaw and listened to what Adrien was saying.

He must give Louis power of attorney for him while he was away, in case he didn't come back. At these words, Jeanne looked suddenly apprehensive, crossed herself, and stood a little closer to her husband. Adrien put a protective arm around her plump shoulders. It was customary in those perilous times, when many a man never came back alive from the wilderness, to bestow power of attorney upon some other member of the family or on a responsible and trusted friend, who would take care of business affairs during the absence, and settle the estate in case he failed to return.

Thus, on April 13, 1669, Adrien Jolliet formally notarized the paper giving his brother control over the former's estate and business affairs. In June he went to Montréal to get supplies to take out to Péré, and left there later in the month.

It was well known to a good many people that Adrien Jolliet was preparing to depart on some unexplained mission, and the Sulpicians in their seminary in Montréal surely heard about it too. The Sulpicians were much interested in the westward push. When the lean, tanned Jolliet, his canoe heavily loaded with food and trade items, paddled swiftly away from Montréal, quite unaccompanied, and went into the first rapids of the Ottawa, the Sulpicians discussed the matter among themselves. They wondered where he was going.

The Sulpicians and the Jesuits had ever been rivals in sending missionaries into the fertile field of the savages of the west. The Jesuits, who had come earlier on the scene, usually found the best spots first, but there still was much country out beyond the horizons of Montréal where there were no priests at all. There was surely room for everyone bound on a holy mission.

When news had come that there were nations living along the great river far to the west who had need of the word of God, the Sulpicians decided to send several of their best men as missionaries to pioneer in that country—and before the Jesuits got there first.

Meanwhile, at the very time that he sent Adrien Jolliet out to check up on Jean Péré and the copper mine, Talon sent a certain Robert Cavelier de La Salle to look for that elusive Great River of which he had had continuing and plaguingly vague rumors. Since, according to La Salle's own self-important account, he was a most proficient woodsman and knew routes of which the Indians had told him, the west-bound Sulpician priests in Montréal decided to throw in their lot with him. La Salle was going in the same direction as they, and numbers would give protection.

The priests—a huge, kindly, ex-soldier turned cleric, Dollier de Casson, and one named M. Barthélmy—were to accompany La Salle. The latter immediately turned the whole thing into a magnificent expedition. Needing soldiers, he secured permission for those who wished to leave the ranks to accompany him. There were to be no less than seven canoes and nearly two dozen men. Anything which La Salle touched seemed to become large and well advertised at once. As was said then: "The expedition made a great noise."

Everyone in Montréal and Québec, in fact, apparently knew all about it. So had Adrien before he quietly departed on his own mission.

But even before the La Salle expedition set off, there had evidently been growing some uncertainty about the man and his changeable nature. Galinée, a Sulpician, wrote:

It occurred to the Abbé de Queylus [the superior at the Sulpician seminary] that M. de la Salle might possibly abandon our gentlemen, and that his temper, which was known to be rather volatile, might lead him to quit them at the first whim, perhaps when it was most necessary to have someone with a little skill in finding his bearings for the return journey. . . . Besides, it was desirable to have some trustworthy map of the route that was contemplated.

So the prudent Abbé de Queylus informed the disappointed M. Barthélmy that he would have to stay behind and that another, René de Bréhant de Galinée, was chosen to go instead, because he knew how to draw a map and was acquainted with the Algonquin language. It would have been even more useful if M. Galinée could have spoken Iroquois, because La Salle, though boasting that he was perfectly acquainted with that language, did not know it at all.

They also discovered with dismay that he had embarked upon this journey almost blindly, and in fact hardly knew where he was going or how to get there. Galinée, perceiving this early, found time to locate someone who did know Iroquois, a Dutchman who, unfortunately, spoke scarcely any French. Though thus linguistically handicapped, they somehow made out with his services.

The La Salle–Sulpician expedition departed July 6, 1669, to seek out the whereabouts of the mysterious Great River. Meanwhile, Adrien Jolliet, knowing his way in the wilderness, went directly to the Lake Superior country.

La Salle's group endured unendingly miserable situations which were largely brought on by the leader's improvidence and the abysmal ignorance which beset members of the party when they were confronted with the no-compromise qualities of wilderness. The priests became ill. Burly Dollier de Casson nearly died of a fever. The food was scarce and very bad. Though they were in the midst of a plentiful land hardly anyone knew how to secure enough to eat.

Instead of following routes which Indians or woodsmen could have shown them, they portaged miles of mud and water and reed swamps where clouds of blackbirds and terns flew up, screeching and darting down to peck their heads. The men waded alder swamps where wiry branches were forever slashing back against the faces of those behind; they endured the incessant attacks of mosquitoes and black flies which were also tormenting the deer and moose of the upper country.

After two and a half terrible, frustrating months of travel, they found themselves, on September 24, only as far as the Ottawa village of Tinawatawa, at the beautiful western end of Lake Ontario.

It seemed to the weary Sulpicians that La Salle was certainly leading them too far from their original goal, from both the big river which none had ever seen and the benighted savages peopling its shores. The party was still traveling, besides, through the missionary field occupied by the Jesuits. It would be unethical for the Sulpicians to settle in this territory, and they were anxious to get to the virgin lands about which they had heard. They were tired and discouraged, mosquito-bitten, tattered, and considerably disillusioned with La Salle, whose irresponsibility had led them into many uncomfortable situations. He wearied them, besides, with his incessant high self-esteem. And they were shocked at his obvious lack of knowledge of the country—he didn't even know how to follow a compass.

The people of Tinawatawa had given them food, and they had eaten and were resting when a lone canoe with one Frenchman and one Iroquois paddled rapidly to shore. The Frenchman, who spoke Ottawa fluently, greeted the people and explained who he was and why he was there. He seemed surprised to find two dozen Frenchmen there ahead of him.

It was Adrien Jolliet. He had already gone up to Lake Superior and was on his way back with an Iroquois who had been held prisoner by the Ottawa to the west. He was returning the prisoner to his own people as a token that the peace which the Ottawa desired to have with the Iroquois was real and sincere.

The Indian in gratitude had shown Adrien a new route which had been unknown to the French . . . by way of Lake Huron, Lake St. Clair, Lake Ontario, and Lake Erie, though Adrien had been forced by the fearful prisoner, who was afraid of falling into the hands of the vengeful Conestoga, to take a somewhat different route overland for part of the way.

La Salle greeted Jolliet with effusive kisses on the cheeks and cordial embraces which left Adrien unmoved. He knew La Salle for what he was. There never had been any friendship between them, partly because La Salle felt that he himself was above such men as the Jolliets who were merchants and traders. But out here in the wilderness, far from Québec and its social distinctions, all Frenchmen were suddenly brothers, and even the imperious La Salle could greet a merchant with affection.

Here, besides, was a Frenchman who spoke many Indian tongues, who knew the wilderness as well as he knew the streets of Québec, and who could assist the travelers on their way. It was a most providential encounter.

The priests eagerly inquired of the way about which Adrien spoke, the lake route. Yes, Adrien said, there was a way. He had also heard, he said, that there was a very numerous nation of Ottawa called the Potawatomi, amongst whom there had never been any missionaries. He said that this tribe bordered on the Iskoutegas and the great river that led to the lands of the Shawnee. Or so he had heard.

Cannily, with these words, Adrien Jolliet, with his Jesuit leanings and his dislike of La Salle, directed the Sulpicians from the way they had originally intended to take, by holding out the bait of unconverted Indians and the lure of a fresh field of missionary endeavor. Instead of helping them on their way to find the virgin territory along the unknown river, he sent them straight into the Jesuit stronghold on Green Bay.

La Salle stood off to one side and his face took on a stubborn, petulant pout. This Jolliet was spoiling his plans, was taking over direction of his expedition, telling him where to go. La Salle's fury mounted. When the priests turned to him to make certain that he was absorbing Adrien's careful directions, they found he had his back to them and was glowering at the shining, placid blue waters of the lake. He kicked at a fly-bitten Indian dog that came too near.

Galinée and Dollier looked at each other in silent understanding.

"Tell us again, carefully," said Galinée, taking out his notebook and a pen, and preparing to make a map. He soon transformed Adrien Jolliet's directions into a chart which would not only tell them which way to go to the place he mentioned, but, even more important, how to get back again.

La Salle refused to go along. He took surly leave of the Sulpicians, with the flimsy excuse that he had decided he must get back to Montréal. Instead, with some of his men, he headed off to the southwest where he later reported that he had found a large river, the Ohio, as it was called by the Indians.

Jolliet went on with his Iroquois prisoner. He was in a hurry to get back to Québec before the season closed in with storms and cold; he must return to report to Talon's lieutenant, Patoulet, about what he had found.

He had, indeed, located Péré, but Péré had not found the copper mine, or so he had said, though Adrien felt that perhaps Péré was not telling all he knew. Ensconced in a bark lodge with an Indian woman, he looked fat, greasy, and happy, and was in no particular hurry to go back to Québec. There was no sign of the thousand-livre subsidy which Talon had mistakenly paid him. He had, however, accumulated a great pile of excellent beaver furs, illegally, of course, because Péré had no license.

Adrien tried to pry out of him the information about the copper mine for which Talon so longed to hear, but Péré was elusive. There might or might not be a rich mine up there, he would say, sucking on his pipe, while the Ojibway woman stirred a pot of rabbit stew and said nothing. Yes, it was true that he had looked. It was very true that there was copper around here. The Indians themselves mined it up along the south shore of Lake Superior, and he waved his hand vaguely to the west; but what good was all the copper in the world itself if you couldn't transport it to Québec?

The pines on the shore where the bark lodge stood gave off a fine fragrance in the summer air; the lake was pale blue, like ice, and there were strange mirages rising above its afternoon horizon, while a cow moose splashed and sloshed with big feet in a reed-grown bay. There were particles of copper and mica glinting in the shallows of the clear lake water where one small wave came in at slow intervals and broke on the multicolored, ice-smoothed, water-worn pebbles. Péré would not tell about the mine.

In vast impatience, but not empowered to drag Péré back to justice, nor knowing quite how he would do it if he had to, Adrien had started for home. He had picked up the Iroquois prisoner, who was grateful to him. For this piece of benevolence, Adrien had been rewarded by learning of the water route Talon also wanted to hear about. In itself, besides, this water route might help to solve the puzzle of the northern mystery, not only for Talon and Colbert and the King, but for others who were curious, too, and who wanted to know what lay beyond the far horizon.

It had been in a spirit of mischief, perhaps of loyalty to his friends the Jesuits, or of dislike for La Salle, that he had sent the gullible Sulpicians up to Green Bay where, he well knew, they would find Father Marquette and Father Dablon in a Jesuit mission field. They would tell them that the place was, indeed, already occupied by very good and capable missionaries.

This is what happened. After taking leave rather thankfully of La Salle, the pair of priests with part of the party went on to Green Bay, while La Salle and the rest went another direction.

The Sulpicians and La Salle at the west end of Lake Ontario were the last Frenchmen to see Adrien Jolliet. He and the Iroquois in the white birch canoe paddled along the shore of the lake. They saw him as he waved a paddle, turning a bit to look back at the village of Tinawatawa and the French who stood watching him go.

Adrien did not come back to Québec. Neither did the delinquent Péré, and La Salle himself was a long time in coming. It seemed to the exasperated Talon that everyone he sent out to the west failed to return. Adrien had been expected early in the autumn; and daily, as October burned gold and scarlet, and as the leaves went down and drifted on the waters of the river carrying them out to the sea, and as the snow geese came again from the Hudson Bay country and went on to no one knew where, Louis, Jeanne, and little Jean-Baptiste, and Zacharie, and Marie, the mother, watched the river and Adrien did not come. Louis, remembering how it had been when the Iroquois captured his brother long ago, and how faith had upheld him during the long days of waiting, tried to hold on to that faith now.

Needing to send a letter to Colbert on the last ship of the season, Patoulet waited until the final possible moment for news. The minister would want to know about these two who had been sent out at considerable government expense to find the copper mine, and who had not returned, not even the reliable and honest Jolliet.

Patoulet wrote:

> Sieurs Jolliet and Péré, to whom M. Talon paid 400 and 1000 livres, respectively, in order that they might go and find out whether the copper mine, which is beyond Lake Ontario and of which you have seen some samples, is rich and easy to exploit, and whether the ore can easily be brought here, have not yet returned. The former should have been back here any day during the whole of last September, and yet, even now, we have no news whatever of him, so that it is necessary to wait until next year before giving you definite information as to how productive the said mine can be expected to be.

The next year when Talon came back, there was still no news of the lost Adrien Jolliet nor of Jean Péré. The latter was very likely living well up on Lake Superior with his Indian wife. But Adrien was dead.

7

~~~~~

MISSION TO THE WEST

WHEN JEAN TALON RETURNED TO QUÉBEC and found that neither Jean Péré nor Adrien Jolliet had brought back any news of the copper mine or had, indeed, been heard from themselves, he determined to wait for La Salle's return before he did anything further in the west. His patience was at an end. Talon would leave Québec for good very soon, when the Count de Frontenac came out as governor of New France. Frontenac was, so gossips said, a bombastic man who was being sent out to the colony to get him away from the court of Louis XIV, where Frontenac had had an affair with the King's new favorite, Mme de Montespan. It would be less embarrassing for all concerned if Frontenac, an outspoken, ebullient man of great charm, went far away. Besides, he and his wife didn't get on very well. Mme Frontenac, a young and beautiful woman, had become deeply involved in court intrigue. In this sort of exciting life a husband was decidedly in the way. Anne Frontenac was a good deal happier when he was elsewhere, so it may have been her pleas, coupled with the King's romance with Mme de Montespan, which banished Frontenac to a post which carried more honor than remuneration, and which definitely removed him from the court and its life.

As Frontenac had been without any very profitable position since the wars were over, he welcomed the post of governor of New France. He expected it to be more inspiriting and challenging work than that of being a hanger-on at court.

But Jean Talon still did not want to give over the fruits of his own Canadian accomplishments to this new man who would be likely to make the most of any glory coming his way. It had been Talon who had ironed out the complexities of a colony which had been falling apart in the dissolute rule of the past: he, Talon, who had brought the pieces together, had made Canada into something of which the King could be proud. Frontenac was going to carry on from here and Talon, selfishly and humanly, did not want him to have the added glory of the discovery of the Mississippi.

It would be one of Talon's own men who would doubtless accomplish this, and for one of these to make a discovery of such portent and do it under the guidance of someone newly come to Canada—it would be insupportable. Talon determined to make one last desperate try for his own fame before he left Canada forever.

When La Salle, whom he had sent to find the river, had not returned by the summer of 1672, Talon could wait no longer. He had waited, hoping daily that La Salle would come, for if he had the news Talon needed, then there would be no reason to send anyone else. But La Salle had not come, and so Talon wearily sought to find the right person to send. He must be the right one this time, not flighty, or irresponsible, or ignorant of the ways of the savages, the wilderness, or the water routes; he must know how to handle men and canoes; how to talk to Indians; how, above all, to make maps. He must know how to survive in the face of hardship and possible disaster, and at all cost bring back news of his discoveries to Talon and the king. There could be no slip this time.

Talon knew whom he would have sent, if the man had lived. That was Adrien Jolliet. None had been better fitted for the task, and he regretted that he had wasted this man in finding out the location of Péré and the mythical copper mine instead of sending him directly to the Mississippi. It was too late now. Somewhere in the wilderness the Sieur Adrien Jolliet was dead.

But the Sieur Adrien's younger brother, Louis, had taken over his brother's work and career, had gone out to the lake country a number of times, hunting news of his brother and carrying on the family business. He had gone west in 1670 with his trade permit and again in 1671. He had spent much time drawing maps and more maps, and at times had come back without enough pelts to satisfy his business associates, but with increasing knowledge of the west. Talon could admit that Louis Jolliet was often a poor businessman, but as an explorer, mapmaker, and man of discernment, judgment, tact, and personal charm, he was perfectly fitted for the task which Talon had in mind. Talon could find good businessmen very easily; it was not so easy to find a good woodsman who was a well-educated man in the bargain.

For he knew that Jolliet was expert in hydrography and the use of the compass and astrolabe. He had had excellent reports of the young man's character and knowledge. Bishop Laval, La Chesnaye, and the Sieur de Lauzon-Charny could not speak highly enough of him. There was something about Louis Jolliet, they would say, which made them admire him with deep devotion. It was that which made the Indians feel kindly toward him, as they had also felt toward Adrien. Thus it seemed to Talon, the more he pondered the matter, that Louis Jolliet should be chosen for this business of determining once and for all just where that great river ran, if it existed at all.

Unfortunately, he could not be subsidized by the govern-

ment. The foreign minister was understandably bitter about
the poor return which he had had from the 1,400 livres
which had been advanced to the unfortunate Adrien Jolliet
and Jean Péré. This time there would have to be some other
arrangement. There was no budgetary fund into which Talon
could dip.

The solution must lie in giving trading rights to Jolliet
and his party. Louis and Zacharie ought to welcome expansion of the family business enterprise. If they should be
given trading and trapping rights in the wilderness they
would enter, it could surely reimburse them for whatever
exertions this Louis would undergo in the King's service. It
did not occur to Talon that the business of exploring the
Mississippi was a full-time job in itself, and that trapping
and trading along the way would be almost impossible, especially bringing back upriver whatever they might secure from
the Indians. To Talon, who had never visited the wilderness
or had ever wanted to, it seemed a fair concession and a
good one which, if handled right, could bring the partici-
pants a pretty sum and, at the same time, work a service
for Talon in finding out what he so desperately wanted to
know at once.

To Louis Jolliet, sunbrowned and swarthy after his summer in the bush country, the proposition was an astounding
one. He was excited, deeply excited, in a way he could not
have expressed. This was what he had wanted, what he and
Adrien had planned for so long and what Adrien now could
never accomplish. Now it was for Louis to carry out the plan
for both of them, and do it not alone for himself and Adrien
but in the service of the King himself!

There was no secret about the impending expedition. He
told the superior at the Jesuit house about it. The superior
was Father Claude Dablon, who, with Father Marquette at
Lake Superior, had desperately wished to find out more about

the marvelous land to the west and south. Both were ardent geographers, explorers at heart, who, by virtue of their posts in the church, were condemned by their own faithfulness to duty to work where the church ordered them. Father Marquette was now at Michilimackinac but Father Dablon had been returned to Québec to become the superior. This was the penalty, the privilege, and the obligation to the Cross; and Dablon accepted it with humility and joy, bitter though the dose sometimes was when his carnal nature cried to run off and adventure through the wonderful wilderness of the west. But he could also rejoice in the good fortune of others, and he, too, was fond of Louis Jolliet. He was at heart still one of the Jesuits, their brother, and Dablon was glad to learn what he would have a chance to do.

When he had heard the young man through, Claude Dablon laid his hand on the other's shoulder. He had a favor to ask.

There was one whom he would like Louis to take with him. Father Jacques Marquette out at Michilimackinac had longed and prayed for the opportunity to discover where the great river flowed and to open missions along its course. There had never been any way in which he could do so before. Since Marquette was fairly expert at mapmaking and adept in certain Indian tongues, he could be useful on the expedition. And Father Dablon explained how it was with Father Marquette, not ordering Louis to take him along, but leaving it up to him. Louis smiled.

He knew and liked Jacques Marquette. He would be glad to take him along. They would all be the better for having a priest to look after their souls. He would have other men with him, strong and experienced canoemen, so that the priest would not have to exert himself to paddle as many of the fathers had had to do when they were on Indian expeditions.

When Claude Dablon had Jolliet's answer, he was as glad as if he himself had been given the chance to go. He wrote a letter to Father Marquette telling him that he was released from his duties at the mission the following spring, whenever Louis Jolliet should come to get him. Marquette was to carry the faith into the distant Indian countries along the mysterious river. He, Dablon, would send a replacement for the mission. Marquette must hold himself in readiness.

Meanwhile, in order to finance his part of the trip and to prevent his business companions from feeling that he was skipping out on a pleasure jaunt, Jolliet pooled his resources with a group of associates, determining beforehand the share of each in whatever profits should result from the trip, to prevent arguments later.

On October 1, 1672, before Giles Rageot, the notary, according to an old document, there "were present Sieur Louis Jolliet; François Chavigny, escuyer; Sieur de la Chevrotiére; Zacharie Jolliet; Jean Plattier; Pierre Moreau; Jacques Largilier; Jean Tiberge; all now of this town, who of their own free will have entered into partnership and society to make together the voyage to the Ottawa country, there to trade with the Indians as profitably as possible."

According to the notarial act, Louis Jolliet bound himself to furnish at his expense all the merchandise, appropriate and suitable goods to carry on trade in the west, as much as they could carry along with them. He was also committed to provide "suitable victuals" to the Sieurs Chavigny, Zacharie Jolliet, Plattier, Moreau, Largilier, and Tiberge and, when they returned from the voyage, to divide all moose, beaver, otter, and marten pelts acquired in the west, according to the prearranged plan. Half of the pelts were to be divided into seven shares, a share for each, and the other half to be for Jolliet himself, since he was paying for all the merchandise, goods, and food and was providing the canoes. He was to have his seventh share also.

The document painstakingly stated that if it was necessary to make presents to the Indians during the voyage, and if some were received in return, they were to be shared by the seven, as well as the money received from the sale of the canoes after their return. The voyage, history-making though it became, was outwardly a purely commercial venture, with men taking part in it solely to make money. Only Louis Jolliet and the priest who would join them at St. Ignace de Michilimackinac, were thinking of something bigger and more grand, an adventure capable of lifting the soul to greater heights than the mere apportionment of so many hides of dead moose and beaver.

Not all the men listed as members of the company went along to hunt for the great river. Seven men, aside from the notaries and not including Marquette, signed the act, while an eighth who was present, Jacques Tiberge, did not sign because he could not write his name. Yet only six of these actually went on the expedition. It is believed that Moreau, Plattier, Tiberge, Largilier, and one other who was hired later on, Pierre Porteret, went on the voyage of discovery with Louis. Zacharie Jolliet very likely was required to stay at Sault Ste Marie to look after the valuable pelts in the warehouse, and the trade goods, supplies, the forge, and other items which could not be left alone to be stolen. He would need to be there to carry on trading. Zacharie may have wanted to go along; it is doubtful that he did.

It was a complicated business, this going on an expedition of discovery and having to finance it himself; it involved so many men and interests and had at the same time so great a chance of risk and failure. It would have been better if the intendant could have subsidized him as he had Adrien. So much depended now upon their getting enough pelts to pay not only for his own high expenses, but to satisfy the partners, not to forget Adrien's widow, Jeanne, now married to the gambler and drunkard, Antoine Baillargé.

Jeanne was not only included in the company operated by the Jolliets, because of her connection with Adrien, but her present husband, in his more sober moments, insisted that she have what was rightfully due her. Louis had neglected to bring back all of the pelts stored at the Sault the year before; Baillargé wanted those pelts and felt that Jolliet was trying to avoid paying his former sister-in-law her share.

Jeanne was fond of Louis. She had often laughed at him for forgetting the serious business of making a living when something more engrossing, like maps, music, or rivers, took hold of his mind. Now she saw how harassed he was with the demands of his partners and with her husband's insisting on past shares being brought to account. She also knew how sadly his funds had been depleted, and so she suddenly offered to lend him a canoe, one of Adrien's, left at Cap-de-la-Madeleine. Louis could use it on the trip and bring back in it those furs which her husband was so eager to lay his hands on.

Louis was grateful to Jeanne. She had always been his friend. Having the extra canoe now required him to purchase only one other. And so finally, on a day in October, 1672, the two crafts, heavily loaded with hundreds of pounds of food, trade goods, beads, knives, hatchets, and bright cheap cloth for the Indians, left Montréal. He had gone to say good-by to his mother in Québec, and to Dablon and Talon and the others who were so much interested in the expedition.

They turned into the rapids of the Ottawa River, the usual way to the lakes, portaged to Lake Nipissing and followed the French River into Georgian Bay. From here one canoe went to Sault Ste Marie and the company's business head-

quarters, while the other, bearing Louis Jolliet himself, paddled across the wind-whipped waters where December cold
already congealed ice in marshes along the shore. A slight
figure in a long, wind-tumbled black gown came out of the
log mission on the north shore as the canoe and its occu-
pants landed. The priest hurried forward, hand out-
stretched, to meet his friend Jolliet.

Marquette was astonished to see him at this late time of
the year when few Frenchmen were roaming the lakes. He
was inordinately pleased to have him there, but when Jolliet
handed him Dablon's letter, an even greater joy began to
grow like a light in his face. Louis smiled, too. It was not
every day that a man had the opportunity to bring such
joy to a friend.

Marquette took both of Louis's hands in his own. He was
so happy that words at first would not come; then they
spilled forth with enthusiasm and delight. He would be
ready whenever Louis came for him, he cried; he could, in
fact, be ready in a trice, this very moment!

But he knew and Louis knew that they could not start
until spring, when the ice had gone out of the lakes. Louis
would spend the winter at Sault Ste Marie, the priest at his
mission. To both of them, however, it was sure to be a very
long winter.

8

~~~~~

THE GREAT RIVER

WINTERS ARE, indeed, long in the upper lakes country. To
Jacques Marquette in the snowbound log mission of St. Ignace de Michilimackinac, and to Louis Jolliet some seventy
miles away at the Sault just below Lake Superior, keeping
busy by trading with the Indians, the interminable winter
seemed never to show any sign of moderating. Instead of a
thaw, there was more snow. Instead of warmth, there was
below-zero cold for weeks on end. To Louis, accustomed as
he was to Canadian winters, this one must have seemed the
most trying of all.

It was not so much the life in the woods. That had become part of him and he liked the personal combat it required merely to keep alive in the cold of the great pine and
hemlock forests around the Sault. But the life indoors was
cramped and dull. He missed music. He missed books. He
missed contacts with educated people. All were far away.
The nights were tedious, and by January conversation had
reached a low ebb of monotony.

Then there came a day when sun shone in a gentler fashion
upon the black-green of the hemlocks. There was a glitter
on the upper boughs of the wind-tossed pines; there was a
subtle smell almost as of growing things, inexplicably coming on the soft wind that was blowing in from the south. The

lake ice thundered in tremendous reverberations when the sun was warm upon it, then, splitting in vast cracks and crevasses, it boomed and moaned all night when the cold returned.

As soon as open water lay bright and dark blue between the crumbling floes, the white gulls came back. The Ojibway women were busy in the maple woods. They had bored holes in the trunks of the big trees, had thrust a little birchbark tube or trough into each hole, with a birchbark pail beneath. The pale sap dripped fast all day when the sun shone, and stopped when the night froze again. The smell of boiling sap over Indian fires filled the woods with a splendid and invigorating perfume. Louis forgot the long winter and breathed deeply the spring aroma of maple sugar and a mild south wind.

It was time at last. The ice broke up in a final abandon which took it out of the open water with haste, only leaving sodden shoals of dark, dirty-looking ice chips heaving up and down in the sheltered bays. The scent of arbutus was in the woods. The maple season was finished, the first young leaves unfolded hesitantly on maple and aspen and birch. The ducks moved north; cock partridges were drumming. It was spring!

Louis Jolliet, together with Jacques Tiberge, Pierre Largilier, Pierre Moreau, Jean Plattier and Pierre Porteret, said good-by to Zacharie, and the party set off, three to a canoe. The seventh member would be the priest. He would change places from time to time, but would not be required to paddle.

The canoes went quickly down the fast waters of the St. Mary River below the Sault, connecting Lake Superior with Lake Huron, and came through the narrow Detour Passage. They followed among the islands of the north shore of Lake Huron, and then suddenly rounded the point where stood

the brown logs of the mission of St. Ignace de Michilimackinac. The warm spring sunshine lay as in a golden aura over
the weathered logs, over the sandy beach, and on the black-
clad figure whose robes whipped in the wind. He shaded his
eyes against the glare. The priest had been waiting for days.

He had everything ready to go. It was swiftly loaded, and
then the men all assembled at the foot of the rough-hewn
log cross standing in front of the mission, and knelt for
prayer. They were quickly on their way. They carried little
food, for they were proceeding south into country where
food would be abundant. Louis had his mapmaking materials, his compass and divider. Marquette had his portable
altar and equipment for celebrating the Mass. He had a
rough map compiled from information given him by the
Indians. The other men needed little save their guns and
ammunition and some brandy.

It is certain, however, that both the priest and Jolliet had
brought their razors in order to be clean-shaven when they
met the Indians along the way. They knew how the Indians
abhorred and scorned men with hairy faces, knew how such
a minor point as this might influence savages for or against
newcomers. Indians had often mistreated and made rude
remarks to the unshaven French explorers, but, because of
the custom of the clergy's shaving, the priests had frequently
found a curious advantage when they were among the less
friendly savages.

It was May 17, 1673, when the two canoes left the
mission of St. Ignace de Michilimackinac, paddled rapidly
out of sight of the few Indians who stood and passively
watched, and were on their way at last.

Louis had mapped their course to follow much the same
route taken many years earlier by Jean Nicolet. It extended
into the lower end of Green Bay, where he had been told

there was a river leading inland to an Indian village. Here they could discover which way to go farther. But on their way they paused for rest and food at a Menominee village near the mouth of the Menominee River. Marquette knew these people; he had been there before.

These were the Wild Rice People. Their staple food was the succulent wild rice which was even then springing up in the shallow waters of river and marsh. The people welcomed the travelers, but feared for them, searching for the Great River. To Jolliet, listening, it seemed that the Indians spoke with such awe that the words should be put into capitals—THE RIVER—as if there could be no other, and that none were greater than this. The river, rising where, flowing into what distant sea?

They could not tell him that. They only knew that it was said to be exceedingly dangerous, full of great whirlpools and savage monsters, and fish as big as a man. Besides all these menaces, the sun was hotter along the river than anything one could possibly imagine. It had twice as much power as here. It scorched men's brains and burned their skins black.

Father Marquette and Louis Jolliet thanked the Indians for their kindly concern and their hospitality, and gave them presents, but Jolliet assured them that his king had sent them to find this river and see where it emptied, and they were bound to obey what he said.

They continued down the west shore of Green Bay to the place where the bay ended and a river, the Upper Fox, took them inland. There was a stop at the Jesuit mission at La Baie, and then they hastened on. The river was shallow and marshy and full of birds; it became so rocky that the men often had to get out and push the canoes forward, with caution and some difficulty because the rocks were sharp and the water cold.

As the men trended ever southwestward, they knew that they were rapidly leaving the French country behind. This was now all Indian territory, the land of the Mascoutens, the Fire Nation. On the map which Marquette had compiled, a Mascouten town lay ahead on the Lower Fox, but although everyone was anticipating it, the first sight of the sprawling collection of bark houses and cooking smokes in a sunny meadow sent a throb of apprehension into the seven men. It was not that they feared the Indians, for these were known to be friendly to white men; it was that this was the jumping-off place, the ultimate limit of discoveries made westward heretofore by the French. What lay beyond this Mascouten community had never been seen by any white man. Jolliet, feeling a surge of excitement at being on the brink of discovery, felt almost as if he were about to see the other side of the moon.

The Frenchmen were given a dignified reception by the Mascoutens and by certain Miamis and Kickapoos who were also there at the time. After the formalities of making speeches, smoking the calumet, and partaking of food of dubious quality, Jolliet broached the subject which was the essential purpose of his stopping here. He would need a guide who could show him and his men the way to the certain portage of which he had been told, which led from the Fox to the river called the Wisconsin. The Frenchmen must rely upon the great knowledge and skill of their friends, the Fire Nation, for assistance.

The chief nodded gravely. It was true, he said: the Frenchmen needed his assistance. He would give them two Miamis who would be their guides.

Next morning they set off at dawn, with the Miamis going ahead in their own canoe. Jolliet was thankful to have them as guides, for the shores were all of a sameness—willows, woods, sand banks, alder swamps. To a Frenchman there was nothing to indicate that a portage was just here, or that it would lead to another river. But at a certain point the Miamis swerved to shore and signaled for the others to follow. The Miamis left their own canoe at the bank and assisted in carrying some of the gear, while the Frenchmen upended the canoes and, two men handling each, carried them on their shoulders up the muddy path.

It might never have been a path at all, but only a muskrat trail or a beaver's drag-route, for all the French could have told. The way grew more soggy underfoot and more over-grown with alders and willows. Clouds of black flies bit until welts were raised on neck and face and arm. The Miamis, oblivious to insects, urged the men on. In all, they went 2,700 paces (Father Marquette himself counted the paces and set the figure down in his journal.) And they came at last to the banks of a strange new river, a river that was silent and shining and amber-colored. It was the Wisconsin at last.

The Miamis waited until the canoes were in the water and were reloaded with the correct balance in each, the men ready at the paddles. The two Indians on the bank raised their hands in a silent farewell, and then they were not there—they had melted into the willows as if they had never been there at all, and the Frenchmen were alone on a river they had never seen before and did not know exactly where it might flow. They had been told only that it emptied into the Mississippi, but how far away the latter was, if it was there at all, no one knew, or even knew how accurate was the description of the course of the Wisconsin. It might carry them far from what they sought. Often the Indians simply fabricated a tale which they decided was what the white men wanted to hear. This was frequently the quickest means of getting rid of them.

Before the party set off again, there was a pause for prayers. The men were impressed with the solemnity of this moment. And then the paddles dipped in unison, and they were on their way down the clear brown waters of the Wisconsin. It had flowed sparkling cold and dark as ale from the cedar swamps and tamarack bogs of the northern wilderness. The sand on the bottom was amber, too, catching the reflection of ripples and the scurrying of water beetles in the shallows, and showing it in transient shadows on the bottom.

As the canoes proceeded, Jolliet and Marquette knew that they had now left the rivers which fed their waters into the Great Lakes and thence down the St. Lawrence to the sea. The Wisconsin flowed southwest, into what sea they did not know. This knowledge, or lack of it, as much as anything else, gave them a feeling of isolation, of greater distance from home, of having severed themselves from the last hold on their home country far away in Canada.

Now and again a deer bounded away from where it had been drinking. There were groups of deer, flicking their white tails against the flies, standing in a glade and watching with their large, dark, white-rimmed eyes as the canoes slid quietly past. And in their eyes was the trusting light possessed by animals of the unharmed wilderness which had never known the disrupting presence of the white man.

Sometimes the canoes startled beavers cutting down young willows. Off on the open uplands, now and again, groups of dark animals grazed, like large cattle, but when the travelers came by chance upon several of these creatures drinking in a muddy cove, and they snorted with a sudden thunder of hoofs, splashing mud and water and kicking sand as they whirled, the men sat back in the rocking canoes and grinned at each other. The wild cattle of the prairies . . . the buffalo, seen now by them for the first time! But how enormous

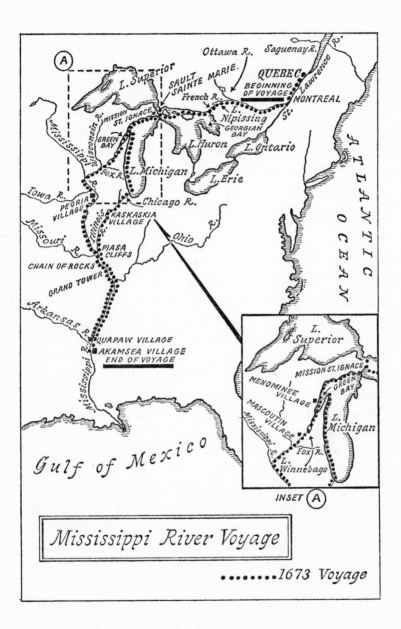

Mississippi River Voyage

.... 1673 Voyage

they were, how splendid. How, the Canadians wondered, did a man ever bring one down with a bullet or, in the case of the savages, with only an arrow or a spear?

On the seventh morning after they had put the canoes into the Wisconsin and had said good-by to the Miamis, a thick fog rolled in over the bottomlands, obscuring a table-land of hills to the rear and hiding whatever lay ahead. Surrounded by a chorus of bird song, the men were awake at dawn. In the willows, the fog hung in droplets of water from every bending leaf, funneling off as from so many little green troughs. The canoes set off again in the chill gray damp.

Then as they rounded a low, densely willow-grown island, the men knew they had come into another river. In spite of the fog, they knew. The waters under them spread more broadly than had the Wisconsin, were darker and stranger. Sheer limestone cliffs were dimly visible on the far shore. There was no doubt in Jolliet's mind that they had come into the Mississippi River at last.

Caught in the gentle current carrying them southward, they let the canoes drift, and even Moreau, Porteret, Plattier, Tiberge, and Largilier, who probably seldom showed much emotion over anything in the landscape, good or evil, must have had almost exalted expressions on their faces. Jacques Marquette looked to the sky where the fog was rapidly breaking and boiling in plumes and wisps, letting the sudden sunshine through to strike apricot and gold on the wraiths, and his lips were moving in prayer. He was smiling as he prayed. This moment was the fulfillment of many hopes and dreams, many hours of poring over maps, and of wondering . . . wondering.

Jolliet in the other canoe had a far-off look in his eyes, a thoughtful look as he trailed his paddle in these strange waters, coming from no one knew where, flowing to no one knew where, and he may have dipped his hand into the Mississippi and solemnly cupped a drink of its water into his mouth. But whether or not he actually did so doesn't matter; for inescapably after that he had the Mississippi forever in his blood.

Marquette wrote: "We entered Mississippi on the 17th of June, with a joy that I cannot express."

Louis Jolliet wrote in his journal, too, but no one knows what he said, for another river claimed his words, his meditations, and his maps. But he needed no written page to remind him of this moment. He had found the Great River.

9

~~~~~~

PEOPLE OF THE MISSISSIPPI

WHEN LOUIS JOLLIET AND JACQUES MARQUETTE charted their
course over the curve of Lake Michigan and down the Fox,
portaged to the Wisconsin and came inevitably to the Mississippi, the voyage had none of the certainty which a look
back upon it might suggest. There was, in fact, no certainty at
all. There was only rumor. Hearsay of Indians and priests,
however, had resulted somehow in a shot in the dark which
miraculously had hit its mark.

Since all previous knowledge of geography ended abruptly
long before the route of the Mississippi was reached, they
had a feeling almost of disbelief that they had found it
so easily. Nevertheless, only geographical ignorance covered
the thousands of miles lying west, south, and north of the
point where the two lone canoes entered the river.

Nor was there, besides, information as to what kinds of
Indians might be expected, or what were their populations,
or where they were located. Therefore, properly anticipating
trouble, as all Canadians must who had had experience with
the Iroquois, there was some trepidation in the explorers as
they set off. They paddled quietly down an unknown river,
bound for no one knew where, through no one knew what
hostile territory and unknown savage strongholds.

✿   ✿   ✿

By 1673, the Mississippi Valley had been the home, fishing waters, and hunting grounds of many scattered tribes since long before the Iroquois lived in Canada. The Mississippi Valley had in fact been inhabited at least eleven thousand years before by the Early Archaic Hunters. They had come, in turn, generation after generation, from still more ancient homes in Utah and Colorado, while their ancestors had arrived during the Ice Age from Siberia. But it had taken the slow passage of time and change to bring any human beings at last to where the Mississippi, still vastly swollen by glacial meltwater, poured to the sea.

But when Marquette had been stationed at Chequamegon Bay on Lake Superior several years earlier, he had been visited by some wandering Peorias, people of the Iliniwek group, who had been displaced by the Iroquois and had gone to live in Iowa. They had begged the priest to come to their people and preach to them. When he had promised to do so, Marquette had had no idea that he would one day be able to fulfill their wish. But now that he was on the Mississippi, he had no way of knowing if he was near the Peoria village or if he had passed it. The Indians had told him that it was not situated on the great river itself, but that a path on the west bank would lead him inland to where they lived.

In all that great unmapped wilderness of the Mississippi, where was a lone path leading to a hidden Indian town?

They had come down the Mississippi for several days without having seen any sign of human life. There was only the placid, beautiful countryside stretching back from the river, the water itself rimmed always with the golden-green of willows with taller cottonwoods behind them. Islands and bottomlands were filled with a jungle of tall trees where herons nested by hundreds. Every dawn the men had seen fog that curled from the water as if in pallid feathers, had seen it glinting in the sun's rays finally piercing it, had known daily a mirror of light on a shining stream. Clouds lay reflected, or, in an impervious gray cover upon the sky, gave to the river a look of ice.

One day dawned wet, but with oilskins over their shoulders they continued paddling in a gray world filled with slanting drops. The willows were drenched and dripping; even the blackbirds were quiet, and the herons hunched somberly on snags and dead trees until the worst was over. By night it had ended, and morning, filled for hours with fog, finally cleared to a day that grew hotter and more humid as the hours wore on.

The hills were green and gentle, with now and again a range of dramatic cliffs rising above broad marshes that filled the space between the course of the river and the hills and bluffs of the valley. Every mile held a changing view. The men were continually fascinated by the beauty and peace of the river, a land without man, wild or civilized. There were only they, the seven, touching their paddles to the water. The sleek birchbark canoes glided along without a sound except the quiet swish of water, the way behind them unmarred or unchanged a moment after they had passed.

It was almost like a dream, Louis had mused, like a reverie, not reality. It was something of the feeling he had had when he sat in the dusky cathedral and played the organ with only himself to hear.

There was nothing harsh or cruel on the river, nothing frightening or ugly; there was only peace. Even the rapids which they had to navigate had been easier than any on the Ottawa. To a people who lived for years in the dread of the Iroquois along the St. Lawrence, this peace in itself held the essence of alarm.

The wildlife interested them. Every day they saw herds of bison and marveled at them—not until they came to the west had the men ever seen one of these incredible creatures. Foraging briefly ashore, the men fired several times into a group of bison and brought one down. They were astounded at the size and weight of this animal. Not all seven of the men tugging and straining together could move its carcass. It had to be cut up where it fell, and the chunks of meat sliced thin enough to dry somewhat in the hot sun, while other pieces were roasted over the fire. Father Marquette made a sketch of the animal before they all got back into the canoes and continued their journey.

The fish in the river were astonishing, too. Once one of the canoes was struck with such violence that the men thought it was a great log coming at them—there were many of these floating menaces—and they righted it in time before shipping much water. Then they saw, just before the thing submerged again, the form of an enormous blue-black fish, shiny as a dolphin, which passed in a slow arc through the water. It was a fish as big as a man, as the Menominees had told them, the giant Mississippi River catfish.

They had been catching sturgeon in their nets to provide food when they couldn't get meat ashore, or when they didn't want to waste bullets which might be needed to save their lives later on. One day, however, Pierre Porteret gave a startled halloo and nearly lost his hold on the net with its heavy, struggling burden. Here was something new and extraordinary—a great, smooth-skinned fish without scales, and with a long, curious spatula terminating its head, almost like that of a swordfish from the sea. It was the paddle-bill catfish, left over from the ancient Age of Fishes. On another day Louis was startled at the sight of a head he saw swimming past. He moved closer to see it better. The thing veered and swam faster. Louis could see that this was neither fish nor turtle, nor yet a fowl of any kind. Incredibly, it was a wildcat bent on reaching the other shore. They let it go, watching as it expertly dog-paddled into the shallows, got to its feet, shook itself like a fur rug freeing itself of a gallon of water, and leaped up among the willows.

But the land and river were too peaceful. Life was never thus for very long. Instead of relaxing in this gentle, idyllic countryside and on the shining river, the men were wary and on guard. At mealtime they feared to make a very big fire on shore, were careful not to make any more smoke than they could avoid. When they were finished they threw the unburned sticks into the water, buried all evidences of fire or bones. They scuffed up sand or mud to hide their footprints, for any savage would know instantly that no Indian had made those tracks.

When darkness fell, they anchored out in the river and spent the night there. For, although they saw nothing to alarm them, they had a watched feeling, as if unseen eyes were upon them, following all their movements. Yet they perceived nothing—no sign of human beings but themselves, no trouble anywhere. Peace . . . it was just too peaceful. Canada had never been like this.

On June 25, Father Marquette cried out suddenly and pointed to the west bank. Footprints of men marked the pliable mud at the brink, converging in a well-beaten path leading from the water's edge up the slope and through the willows. Louis directed the canoes to be paddled to the shore. They cautiously landed.

This, surely, must be the place, Marquette was exclaiming in excitement, must be the way to the Peoria village to which he had faithfully promised to come. He was here at last.

The five canoemen were astounded at the plan as Louis explained it. They were to stay in the canoes, remain out in the river as much as possible, and be ever watchful. If by some chance the two found unfriendly Indians and were captured and slain, then the five were to wait no more than three days, and not to come in search of them. If they were not back by then, he and the priest would surely be dead, and the five were to go back at once to Québec and report to Talon.

On silent moccasins, the priest and the explorer, carrying a bag of gifts, went up the mud-packed trail. They disappeared among the willows, then reappeared as the disconsolate and pessimistic men on the river watched them growing smaller in the distance, and then lost sight of them.

The two walked for what seemed a long time. The day grew hot and the recent rain brought about a growing humidity which was most uncomfortable to men from the north. Perspiration rolled down their tanned faces. Marquette now and again fanned himself with his hat. Jolliet opened his shirt to the waist.

Meadowlarks sang and grasshoppers buzzed and leaped in the heat. Finally, several hours later, as the two neared a small river, they saw an Indian village on the slope. They had come so quietly that not even the dogs were aware of them, so near the two could hear Indians talking among themselves. It would be unwise to startle them. If they were mistaken for spies and enemies they would probably be shot first and questioned later.

Jolliet raised his powerful voice and Marquette with considerable vigor joined in. Then they stopped, waited for the sudden racket to take effect. Men, women, children, and dogs tumbled out of the cabins. The dogs made a deafening row, and then everyone but the dogs paused at sight of the two strangers standing in the trail.

The dogs got their second wind and came charging forward. They were yelled at in violent Indian command and drew back, tails down, still alert with teeth bared. While Louis and the priest stood waiting, four old men came forward to greet them. Two carried long tobacco pipes ornamented with carving and decorated with dangling feathers and shells. The four walked with dignified slowness tempered with caution, and raised the pipes at intervals to the sky, as if offering them to the sun itself. A wisp of smoke curled from each pipe. No word was said; there was only this eloquent gesture of raising the calumets as the men came forward.

Marquette, speaking in the Illinois tongue, asked the four if they were indeed of that tribe, and was immensely relieved to learn they were the displaced Peorias he sought. The four old men, reassured in turn by the visitors' knowledge of their language, offered them the pipes to smoke. The tobacco was acrid and vile, the smoke gagging, but the two obediently put the pipes to their lips, and nodded pleasantly to their hosts. The preliminaries over, the welcoming committee invited the newcomers to the village.

At the door of the cabin in which they were to be entertained, Louis and the priest were greeted by a very old man who stood erect, stark naked, with his wrinkled arms extended and lifted toward the sun as if he wished to protect himself from its summer rays. In slow, ringing tones, the old man said, as Marquette later reported it: "How beautiful the sun is, O Frenchmen, when thou comest to visit us! All our village awaits thee, and thou shalt enter all our cabins in peace."

Then the old man stood aside with dignity, and the two entered the cabin. Inside it was stifling hot and stinking on that June day. The people, packed in tight rows around the walls, were completely silent as the two entered, but they devoured the visitors with their eyes, as if they could not look enough at them, or admire them enough, or be reverent enough before these marvelous creatures from another world. Reverence caused their silence; it was the greatest compliment and tribute they could pay.

But now and again the silence was broken as Marquette heard them say in low tones: "How good it is, my brothers, that you should visit us."

The two were no sooner seated and given the calumet to smoke again, than the old man announced that the great chief of all the Illinois wished to hold council with the visitors, and they were to be conducted to his town which was at some distance. So Louis and Father Marquette, though somewhat weary and very warm, went off with their hosts across a grassy, flower-strewn prairie, while the Indians of the village, who had never seen a Frenchman before, would not be left behind. They could not be disrespectful by openly staring, so they came along through the deep thickets of giant blue-stem grass, hurried ahead, dropped down and then appeared suddenly in front of the Frenchmen, raised up high enough to take a good look, then scuttled off to the rear, or ahead again to come up for another quick look. They lay in the grass along the trail, they followed quietly and gazed, and were gone like rabbits, all noiselessly and with the greatest respect and awe.

The chief of the Illinois was waiting for them. He was flanked by two of his old men, all three very erect and naked, holding the calumet to the sun, and again Louis and Father Marquette had to smoke it. They could still taste the last two pipes they had had to endure.

Inside the large cabin of the chief, Marquette was delegated to speak to the assembled Indians and offer presents. He assured the people that the great captain of all the French had indeed subdued the terrible Iroquois, so that the

Peoria could now go home again to the Illinois River. Then he asked the old question: *Where does the great river flow? How far to the sea?*

They could not tell him. They had not lived long enough near the Mississippi to know very much about it, except that downstream there were terrible figures painted on a cliff, designs which held an evil magic. They knew that there was a certain demon below which ate up canoes and men.

When the chief had finished explaining about the river, he signaled a little boy about nine years old to come to him. He was solemn and black-eyed, his hair cut in a bristly scalp lock, a beaded loincloth around his narrow, copper-colored hips. The chief spoke again:

> I thank thee, Blackgown, and thee, O Frenchman, for having taken so much trouble to come to visit us. Never has the earth been so beautiful, or the sun so bright, as today; never has our river been so calm, or so clear of rocks, which your canoes have removed in passing; never has our tobacco tasted so good, or our corn appeared so fine, as we now see them.
>
> Here then, is my son, whom I give to show thee my heart.

And the chief presented the little boy to Louis Jolliet, and gave to Marquette a calumet of polished gray pipestone as a passport to the nations down the river. For, if the Frenchmen insisted upon going into these terrible places, they must take this protection along, which was the strongest power he could give them. The calumet was a sign of peace among all men.

There followed an elaborate feast. Louis and the priest, as honored guests, were not permitted to feed themselves. The master of ceremonies took over this task, first blowing upon the food to cool it before it was put into their

obediently opened mouths. The first course was contained
on a large wooden platter, and was composed of sagamité,
cornmeal boiled in water and seasoned with rancid fat. This
was followed by a large roasted fish, from which the master
of ceremonies carefully removed the bones before feeding
the guests. This dish was followed by a whole roasted dog.
This had to be refused. As politely as he could, and with
obvious regret, while Marquette averted his eyes from the
distressing sight, Jolliet explained that although the roast dog
was undoubtedly delicious and well cooked and a great
treat, it was against the custom of the French to eat this
kind of meat, and they must be excused.

When Marquette translated, the Indians, who had many
food taboos of their own and did not question this, removed
the roast which was doubtless consumed by those outside.
The final course, however, was not only tasty but well cooked
and agreeable. The Indians had been on their summer
buffalo hunt and had taken a young bull. The roasted hump,
a delicacy, was pulled apart by the master of ceremonies,
the pieces cooled by his breath, and the fattest morsels put
into the mouths of the guests.

Later, without a chance to rest, they were taken on a tour
of the town. It consisted of nearly three hundred houses
and very few were missed on the tedious rounds of inspec-
tion.

Father Marquette was happy. He went about blessing
everyone he met on the tour, and later he offered the holy
Sacrifice. Meanwhile, wherever they went the people gave
them presents—belts, garters, mats, and small items made
of bear and bison skin. None had any money value. Jolliet,
remembering wryly how his business partners had insisted
on a share in all the gifts, decided they would have been
disillusioned by the quality of presents which Indians cus-
tomarily gave to visiting dignitaries. Looking back, Québec

and the petty haggling there before the trip seemed as remote as another world.

The two slept that night in the chief's cabin. The next day,
after Father Marquette celebrated Mass, they departed for
the river. They were considerably encumbered by now with
miscellaneous Indian presents, and were accompanied as
well not only by the chief and his officials but by everyone
in both villages. Some six hundred people followed in a
great crowd over the hot prairie. The little Indian boy who
had been given to Louis stayed close at his father's side.

When the five men waiting in growing anxiety with the
canoes caught sight of this horde of savages advancing upon
them, they were about to paddle hastily away to escape
what appeared to be certain massacre, when they saw that
Louis Jolliet and Father Marquette were in the vanguard
and were obviously unharmed and happy.

The little Indian boy had been very quiet all the way
down to the shore. Louis tried to persuade the chief to keep
his son there, but the chief insisted that he should go with
the exploring party. From the canoe where he had been
given a seat, the boy followed with his eyes the receding
shore where his people stood marveling at the curious white
craft. He did not cry, though his black eyes had a stony,
desperate look. Louis, understanding, gave him a bit of
maple sugar from his pouch and let him paddle for a while.

From that point onward, there grew between the man
and the boy a deep and happy affection. The boy—and
Jolliet in his writings never gave his name—became an
accepted member of the party. He was quick to learn. Jolliet began to teach him to read and write and to speak
French, which the boy picked up so rapidly that he was
soon chattering away in the new tongue. Father Marquette,
delighted with the lad's aptitude, commenced instructions
in the catechism.

A few miles down the river, Jolliet, with the full consent of the disgusted Moreau, Largilier, Tiberge, Plattier, and Porteret, quietly disposed of most of the Indian gifts in the river. They were of no value. The party could not be burdened with so much, though Jolliet and Marquette kept an item or two to bring back as a souvenir.

10

~~~~~~

AN END TO PEACE

BOTH THE MENOMINEES AND THE PEORIAS had warned the
explorers of demons in the river and of the evil powers contained in certain pictures of dragons on cliffs downstream.
The men, however, had begun to feel that the lovely, placid
river and its myriads of islands would provide no basis for
the rumors and dread warnings when, soon after they had
passed the mouth of the Illinois River and come abreast of
a tall palisade of undulating white and buff limestone cliffs
on the east bank, they saw the first of the so-called menaces.

The Indian boy was afraid and would not look at the
rocks, but Marquette and Jolliet and the others stared with
amazement at the pictographs high above them. Marquette
described them thus:

> While skirting some rocks, which by their height and
> length inspired awe, we saw upon one of them two painted
> monsters . . . upon which the boldest savages dare not look,
> or rest their eyes. They are as large as a calf; they have
> horns on their heads like those of a deer, a horrible look,
> red eyes, a beard like a tiger's, a face like a man's, a body
> covered with scales, and so long a tail that it winds all
> around the body, passing above the head and going back
> between the legs, ending in a fish's tail. Green, red and
> black are the three colors composing the picture. Moreover,
> these two monsters are so well painted that we cannot be-

lieve that any savage is their author; for good painters in France would find it difficult to paint so well—and, besides, they are so high up on the rock that it is difficult to reach that place conveniently to paint them. Here is approximately the shape of the monsters as we have faithfully copied them.

And Father Marquette made a sketch in his journal to show what the monsters looked like. Much later they were known as the Piasa Bird, but no one else evidently made a portrait of them, and Marquette's picture, as well as the one which Jolliet no doubt made, was lost. No one knows exactly what the explorers saw. The pictures on the rocks themselves have long since been destroyed.

A menace far more real than the mythical creatures on the cliff met them not many more miles downstream. On the west bank, the tumult and rush of the Missouri River came in to join the Mississippi. The former brought with it the thick clays and paint-colors from the deserts and badlands, from the Rocky Mountains themselves, from the land of the Yellowstone and beyond.

The Pekistanoui, as the Indians called this river, must have been flooding from a great rain somewhere up in the mountains or out on the plains, for in June it does not normally come in with such a turmoil as Marquette described:

> We heard the noise of a rapid, into which we were about to run. I have seen nothing more dreadful. An accumulation of large and entire trees, branches, and floating islands, was issuing from the mouth of the river Pekistanoui, with such impetuosity that we could not without great danger risk passing through it. So great was the agitation that the water was very muddy, and could not become clear.

But somehow, by hugging the east bank of the Mississippi, they got around the tumbling mud and debris and past a couple of dead buffaloes washed down from the plains. Jolliet and Marquette looked back, long and searchingly, wondering where this obviously great and powerful yellow-brown river originated. In many ways it was far wilder and larger than the Mississippi itself, which, they had even now begun to suspect from the generally southward direction in which they had been traveling, could empty only into the Gulf of Mexico. The Missouri, however, was coming from the west in such a manner as to lead them to feel that this, perhaps, was the real course to pursue—the long-sought river which would lead them to the Pacific Ocean.

But they had been commissioned to explore the Mississippi, not the Missouri, no matter how alluring the latter might be. The mystery and wonder held them, however, and they thought about the Missouri for a long time.

The two canoes bounded on the tumbling current passing through the Chain of Rocks. Farther downstream they had to paddle fast and well to keep upright as they went between the standing pillars of the Grand Towers. The river quieted after that, speeding them in great sweeps down to the place where the Ohio came in, then faster still upon an incredibly wide expanse of water which was the lower Mississippi. The river had been broad enough before to merit the name of Great River, but now Jolliet with awe could see why it really deserved that title. The muddy waters, discolored by the Missouri, stood separate from the green waters of the Ohio, until at last they all mingled and became one. By the time the canoes had reached the Chickasaw Bluffs of Tennessee, the river had become a great chocolate-colored flood creamed with whitecaps stirred up by the wind.

Everywhere the driftwood was a terrible trial and danger. Jolliet had seen none anywhere to equal it. Whole trees with jagged, broken boughs like lances floating on the powerful current bobbed and surged with great violence and almost animallike vigor; they were impossible to turn aside

and very difficult to avoid. The canoemen had to be continually watchful lest one of these monsters come up from
behind and ram the canoes. The other men were obliged
to keep a careful eye forward for the telltale shimmer in
the water; this would indicate a submerged snag fastened
in the mud which, with horrid ease, could rip the bottom
out of a canoe.

They had to watch for great eddies which churned out
from coves along shore and ate into the soft mud and sand
of the banks with incredible power, catching whole trees in
a slow and tremendous whirlpool that carried masses of pale
brown foam. A canoe could never get out of an eddy like
one of these, a hundred feet wide and cupping downward
with a terrifying implication of doom.

None had ever seen anything like this river. The Ottawa
and the St. Lawrence were mild in comparison. It seemed
unbelievable that this lower Mississippi should be all a part
of that same placid, shining stream into which they had
come only a few weeks ago.

But with the exception of an unexpected party of Shawnee near the mouth of the Ohio, the French had seen no
more Indians until, passing down the Arkansas shore and
dodging snags and suffering in the heat, a sudden cacophony
of yells and war whoops broke out on the bank. The canoes
were almost abreast of a large Indian town before the men
realized it was there, though their progress down the river
may well have been watched and followed for miles without their knowledge.

The racket was definitely hostile. A swarm of arrows flew
out but fell harmlessly like rain around them. Marquette
invoked the aid of the Blessed Virgin; the men paddled
faster. Taking turns with free hands, they cocked their
loaded pistols. Savages were swarming to the water's edge
and hurling stones and chunks of wood. And the noise was

so much like that of the Iroquois on the war path that every man shuddered with a deep wrench of inner fear.

If they could cut across the river and bypass the ugly commotion, they might have a chance. But before they could go far, several long cottonwood dugouts, loaded with naked warriors armed with bows and arrows and spears, shot out from shore. One of the canoes closed in from behind while three more went downstream to intercept and capture the two little birch canoes from Canada. Some overly eager young men who found no room in the dugouts leaped into the water in an atttempt to swim out to assault and capsize the Frenchmen, but were turned back by the current.

The French were trapped. Louis gave orders, however, not to fire until there was no other recourse. Marquette meanwhile was bravely lifting the calumet over and over, and continued to wave it vigorously to attract the attention of the yelling savages. They, however, were too infuriated to notice anything but the two strange white craft which were now being towed to shore with more wild whoops and ugly yells of insult and triumph. The men, remembering things that had happened to people who had had the misfortune to be captured by the Iroquois, prayed.

But, once ashore, and jostled and knocked about by their captors, Marquette still lifted the calumet in their very faces, until at last its magic began to work.

One of the old men, less hotheaded and blindly excited than the braves, suddenly became aware of the calumet.

With shrill exclamations he ordered the young men to desist. "Honor the calumet," he screeched, pointing to Marquette and the pipe the Peorias had given him. Reluctantly, the warriors halted as they were preparing to bind the seven to trees and stakes. Another old man joined the first and the two harangued violently; some of the young men still scowled and gripped their weapons with intent to use them.

The old men then boldly wrenched the weapons from the hands of the braves and threw them eloquently into the canoes, then turned to apologize to the visitors.

Jolliet drew a long breath of relief. Marquette gave silent thanks to God and his Protectress, and the men began to feel more confident of living for a while longer. Jolliet could think of a good many other places in which he would have preferred to stay for doubtful hospitality than among these furious people who, he learned, were Quapaws, but there was nothing to do now, whether friendly or not. There was no choice. The Indians had them.

The language spoken by the elders was quite unknown to Marquette, even with his fluency in six Indian dialects, so they had to speak by signs, the best way they could. There were blank looks, then dark looks and a growing murmur among the people. They obviously thought the newcomers were lying. It was impossible for them to have come from so far away, not in those incredible craft. A brave, with a sneer, thrust his spear through one of the canoes, and Pierre Moreau with an exclamation of horror leaped to protect it from being mutilated. These two canoes were the one link the expedition had with home and Canada. The Indian laughed scornfully and again thrust his spear through the birchbark.

Attention, however, was thus diverted from the captives themselves to the canoes. The people gathered around to examine them and the strange white covering on the queer, narrow craft. They asked by signs what animal bore a skin like that, and looked incredulous again when Marquette patted a nearby sycamore trunk, not as white as a birch, to explain that the canoes were made from the bark of a similar but smaller tree.

The braves scowled again at such obvious lies and poked a hole in the other canoe. The boats would shortly have

been no better than sieves if a very old man had not come
slowly up to the group. Age was respected even among the
scornful Quapaws, and they fell back for him to look at the
canoes, too. But he had not come to see them. He had heard
words spoken which he had not heard for many a moon and
had come to greet the man who uttered them.

The old man was of the Illinois Confederacy, a Mitchigamea who, with some of his people, had fled southward
when the Iroquois came down the valley, and had sought
refuge with the Quapaws. The other Mitchigameas had
gone on, leaving him there, and he had not heard his native
tongue spoken for a long time. He was glad to be able to
speak to someone who knew what he was saying.

While Marquette with thankfulness plied the old man
with questions, Jolliet passed out presents to the elders.
Pierre Moreau and Jacques Tiberge, muttering quiet but
black imprecations through their beards, got out the resins
and sinews and patches to mend the desecrated canoes,
while the Quapaws, wide-eyed and unhindering, watched
the process. The little Indian boy from upriver, solemn-eyed,
observed everything and listened to Marquette and the
elder.

Marquette explained their mission on the river. He asked
where the river flowed, and how far was the sea. But the
old man did not know. He relayed the query to some of the
others, but they did not know, either. They assured Jolliet
and Marquette, however, that there was an Akamsea village
a little way down the river, another Quapaw group, where
they might indeed learn all they wished to know of this
thing called the sea. Sending unwelcome visitors with un-
answerable or embarrassing questions to a farther place for
a possible answer was an old Indian trick.

Trick or not, Jolliet was only too eager to leave this hostile
place, and would have set off at once if the canoes had been

mended. He did not trust the hotheaded young warriors who had so nearly taken their lives and who, given half a chance, might easily finish the job. Yet to leave at once, even if the canoes could travel, might be to invite further anger, so they reluctantly stayed. Even now the Quapaw women were preparing a feast of the usual sagamité and roasted fish.

But the night on shore was passed in sleepless uneasiness.

Next morning, escorted by ten savages in a heavy cottonwood canoe, the party set off for the Akamsea village which lay on the east bank of the Mississippi, almost opposite to the place where the Arkansas River entered the former stream.

The Akamsea, evidently warned that they were to have guests, were ready for them. A welcoming group presented the calumet and escorted the Frenchmen up the slope to the village, while the Quapaws returned home. In the Akamsea village, canopies had been erected to keep off the furious July sun, and finely woven mats were placed on the ground as seats for the visitors. The elders sat in front of them, while the people arranged themselves in loose semicircles outward. There was an interpreter who spoke Illinois better than the old Mitchigamea. Marquette was grateful. He asked the old burning question: *How far to the sea?*

This time he had an answer. Yes, the Quapaws knew about the sea. It was only about ten days' journey downriver, but the Quapaws seldom went there now because fierce nations dwelt in those parts and traded with the Europeans. Through trading, however, the Akamsea had come into possession of European-made knives, beads, and hatchets. Jolliet asked leave to examine some of these. His trader's eye told him that they could not be of French manufacture, nor yet English, but Spanish. Yes, undoubtedly Spanish. He told this to Marquette, and then his deduction

was confirmed when the interpreter went on to say that
there were certain Blackgowns who rang little bells and
knelt to pray.

Jolliet saw Marquette turn pale. He translated the news
to Louis, and Louis to his men. The Spanish—at the end of
the Mississippi!

So what they had been suspecting was true. The Mississippi was actually the same river which the Spanish had
claimed a century before, De Soto's *Rio del Espiritu Santo*.
For some days, Jolliet had been resigned to this fact, for his
compass and daily readings of the sun and the course of the
river had convinced him. But now that it was verified, the
blow was nonetheless bitter.

To equivocate was impossible. The fact remained that
Spain was an enemy to France. For seven Frenchmen, virtually unarmed, to venture into that stronghold, even if only
bent on determining the exact route of the river, could mean
capture or death.

After the lengthy feast and many speeches laboriously
translated by the interpreters, the guests had gone to bed
in the chief's large, airy, mat-hung house and all were asleep
but Marquette and Jolliet. They had waited until now to
discuss what they should do next, in the light of the news
of what lay down the river, when a sudden turmoil broke
out in the village. The angry tones of the chief haranguing
someone with vehemence rose into the quiet night. A greater
glow of the fire in the council circle came simultaneously
with the sudden appearance of an Indian at the door of the
lodge. He beckoned to the Frenchmen to come at once. The
priest and Jolliet steeled themselves for what might happen
next.

They saw the chief at a distance. He stood naked, like a
bronze statue, very tall, very still, behind the leaping flames.
His arms were uplifted and his hands held the calumet. As

Jolliet and Marquette approached the fire, he began to speak
in dramatic and vivid sign language, augmented by asides
from the sleepy, hastily summoned interpreter. The chief
said with dignity that he had just learned that villains had
been plotting against the guests to rob them and take their
lives, and that he, the chief of the Akamsea, had been
deeply offended by this breach of his hospitality. He would
thereupon dance the calumet to show that he meant only
good to them.

Jolliet and Marquette seated themselves warily to watch
and wait for what would follow.

In the red blaze of the fire and against the purple black-
ness of the warm southern night, in the presence of the
quickly assembled Akamsea, the chief danced. He raised
the calumet to the stars, put the stem to his mouth and drew
a mouthful of smoke, let it rise to the sky. Now he began to
move in a splendid rhythm to the beating of a drum. Then
he presented the pipe to each guest, never losing the beat
of the rhythm or the solemn feeling of awed mystery surrounding his glistening body which perspiration made to
shine, in the heat of the fire and the steaming, humid night,
as if it were made of polished metal.

*Beat—beat—beat—bow low with the calumet—rise, turn,
leap, turn,* the timing never missed the thumping heartbeat
of the drum. The cadence changed, the drum pounded
faster. The chief twisted . . . parried . . . thrust as if the
calumet were a spear and he were dueling with an adversary,
leaping with the sinuous grace of a ballet dancer. Now there
rose a singing among people in the background, a chant
that was like musical instruments muted in the night, a wail,
a calling to something the French could neither see nor
comprehend. But they felt a strange prickling along their
spines and the hairs rose on their necks, as the chief leaped

faster as if pursued by demons, in strange *pas de chats* and *arabesques.*

The drum stopped like a heart stilled by death. The voices died. The fire was low. The chief stood, transfixed, his bronzed body dripping, and he began to speak.

Then he handed the calumet to Jolliet, and to Marquette. The chief was on their side. Against plotters and assassins, they were now protected.

But how safe they really were, and for how long, they could not tell. Back in the darkness of the house allotted to the party, the two could not sleep. The incident had stirred them more than either would admit. The primeval fury, the animal grace, the ritualism, the symbolism of the calumet dance, the languorous atmosphere and fragrance of a southern night with unknown forest depths standing behind and the occasional glint of the Mississippi in starlight beyond; the fire; the voices; the drum; the dark houses of unseen Akamsea—which ones had been the hostile ones?—here was something strange and new and wild and infinitely stirring to the blood.

They lay on their mats and talked. They listened for warning noises, but there were few sounds after the people went back to their houses. The eerie voice of a bird, the chuckwill's widow, coughed in the forest, and something that could have been a panther yowled and squabbled with another. There was an owl calling somewhere in the riverside trees; an incessant racket of night insects left no real silence in the darkness.

The result of that evening was what they both knew must come. The decision was a cruel blow to their adventurous spirits, but duty was stronger. They must turn around now and not follow the Mississippi to its end. Short of their goal by how many leagues they could not be sure, they must go back while they still had their papers, their notes, their maps, and could report what they had found to Talon and Frontenac, who, in turn, could inform Colbert and the King about the fact that the Mississippi did not flow into the Great South Sea, but into the Gulf of Mexico.

Louis Jolliet and Jacques Marquette were intelligent, disciplined men of good judgment. It was these traits which caused them to be selected for this mission, and it was these traits which triumphed now in spite of their personal inclinations to adventure south to see where the river actually emptied. The next day was Sunday. Marquette could celebrate the Mass here, and on Monday morning at dawn they would start back.

11

~~~~~~~~~~

THE ILLINOIS COUNTRY

THE WAY BACK was much harder than had been the 1,100 miles between the mouth of the Wisconsin and the mouth of the Arkansas. Paddling up the Mississippi meant fighting the river every foot of the way, for the water, by July, was low. Great sandbars, baking in summer heat like slabs of Indian cornbread, jutted out of the water as desert islands, with only a few willows on some that had been above water long enough to support life. Along the drying shores herons fished. Cormorants dived. The vultures endlessly circled their sinister shadows over sand and mud and water, over willows and cottonwoods shimmering in heat, and over the red clay of the bluffs.

The canoes had to pick their way, hugging slack water along shore wherever the bars and snags would let them. In low water the snags themselves, great uprooted trees lodged in the mud, were a constant menace. If ever the French brought ships to the Mississippi, as Jolliet was already planning, some means must first be devised to remove the execrable snags before any navigation could be safe.

They were glad when they had passed the mouth of the Ohio. Travel was easier above this point. They found it easier still above the Missouri; then, following the suggestion of the Peorias, they turned into the mouth of the Illinois River. It provided a short cut, the Peorias assured them, to Lake Michigan. The Peorias had also said that, now that the Iroquois were reported to be gone from the valley, the displaced tribes might come back to their old haunts along the Illinois and, if so, might see the explorers there.

The Illinois River charmed the voyagers as not even the upper Mississippi had delighted them. The Illinois was the loveliest river they had ever seen. It was gentle and broad, not at all fierce, with prairies and woods and low hills extending back from it in splendid vistas lying around every gentle bend. Bison, elk, deer, and other animals were abundant and unafraid. There were great flocks of wild pigeons and parakeets, wild swans and ducks and herons, and there were many beaver. To find the beaver gave the French a feeling of gladness, of coming home. They had seen no beaver down the Mississippi. The Quapaw and Akamsea, benighted souls that they were, had never even heard of a castor or knew what it was like, nor what this animal meant to white men and Indians of the north.

But now there were beaver along the meadows and marshes of the Illinois, and, in many places, great waving beds of wild rice. The more Jolliet saw of this fine country, the more he fell in love with it. While the canoes passed up the river, he was even then beginning to plan on coming back with a party of men to clear and colonize. One would not have to spend ten years in routing trees, stumps, and rocks in order to have prosperous farms in this fertile country with its long growing season, as a man did in Canada. He would be self-sufficient, except for the matter of salt, and he could surely solve that problem. There might even be natural licks in this country; the deer and bison would lead him there.

Jolliet promised himself that as soon as he could, with due permission from the King, he would come back and live in the Illinois country. In all his travels he had never seen any place he liked so well.

They paused for a day or two at a large Kaskaskia town beneath a bold sandstone bluff, then continued their way with some of the Kaskaskia going along to show them the route to where the Illinois River forked into the Des Plaines. The Indians stayed with them until they crossed the portage to the Chicago River, which took them quickly to the wave-beaten sands of Lake Michigan itself.

Louis had been thoughtful as they portaged the canoes and baggage to that next river. It was not really very far, and he was thinking with growing excitement how easily a canal might be cut between the Chicago River and the Illinois, making one long waterway to connect the Mississippi and the Gulf of Mexico with Lake Michigan and the St. Lawrence.

Later, when he told Dablon about the journey, he said:

> . . . we could easily sail a ship to Florida; all that needs to be done is to dig a canal through half a league of prairie from the lower end of Lake Michigan to the River of St. Louis [the Illinois]. Here is the route that we would follow: the ship should be built on Lake Erie, which is near Lake Ontario; from Lake Erie it could easily pass to Lake Huron and thence to Lake Michigan. The canal which I mention would be dug at the end of the latter, connecting it with the River of St. Louis, which empties into the Mississippi, which the ship could easily descend to the Gulf of Mexico.

He had been tremendously fired by this plan as the canoes reached Lake Michigan on the homeward journey. He was eager to tell Count de Frontenac, who would surely be interested. To open a waterway between the upper Great Lakes and the Gulf of Mexico might compensate Canada and Talon for Jolliet's failure to find a western route to the Pacific.

Proceeding up the Lake Michigan shore, portaging at Sturgeon Bay into Green Bay, they reached Mission St. Xavier by the end of September, 1673. They had neither lost a man nor had run into any serious danger, barring what might have happened with the hotheaded Quapaws and Akamseas.

Father Marquette was ill. For many days on the long and exhausting river journey he had suffered recurring bouts of dysentery, and sometimes they had had to delay the journey a day or so while he rested on the shore. It is probable that he remained at the mission while Louis and at least some of the men, and the Indian boy, went on to reach Sault Ste Marie before winter. Louis was anxious to see what had been happening up there in his absence, and to discover how Zacharie had made out with the business.

It was too late to go back to Québec this fall, but he would improve the time at the Sault during the winter by writing up his notes more fully and perfecting his map. It had been sometimes difficult to draw a map while he was in a canoe, and there was no place on shore, except for an occasional level rock layer, to provide smooth drawing space. He would polish both map and notes, and make copies which he would leave at the Jesuit mission at the Sault before he went home in the spring. Thus if anything happened to the originals, the copies would be safe. Impatient though Jolliet was to get back at once and tell of his finds and deliver his map, it was wiser to wait and be sure of getting there. It was also very important to secure as many pelts as possible during this winter, as he had during the previous one, to help defray the expenses of the trip.

And so it was in early spring, as soon as the Ottawa was open, that Louis Jolliet set out from Sault Ste Marie. Two men were with him, which two we do not know; they might not have been any of those who had gone on the expedition.

And the Indian boy was with him, together with a load of pelts tied in neat flat bundles, and a small chest containing his map and journal, his navigation instruments and souvenirs of the journey. Day by day in the pleasant, cool spring they paddled down the St. Mary River to Lake Huron. He wondered how Father Marquette was doing, and if he had come back to St. Ignace, but there wasn't time to go there now to find out. He must get to Québec. He had tarried far too long already.

The Ottawa was galloping with snow-water. Its dangerous rapids were leaping white in dangerous, churning cascades, but it was the shortest way home, the customary route to take. The canoe with the three men and the boy, and the precious chest and pelts, hastened over the rapids and had passed through forty-one of them, nearing Montréal at last. The Indian boy had laughed at the excitement of the wild blue-and-white water, and the Frenchmen laughed, too, singing boisterous songs of the *coureurs des bois,* and kept their paddles going in expert command of the canoe in the racing river.

And then in the forty-second rapid they hit a rock. The canoe leaped into the air . . . capsized . . . and men, boy, canoe, and chest disappeared into the turmoil of white water.

Fishermen seldom or never went into the rapids just above Montréal. The rough water made fishing difficult or impossible. But on a day in July, 1674, there were fishermen at this spot and they saw, suddenly, a body tossed on the tumultuous water, then lost sight of it. They came out on the rocks and there discovered a limp form cast across a boulder, head and hands in the water, legs still immersed, the body about to be swept off again. The men leaped forward, slipped, almost fell, but pulled the body out of the way of the water and laid it on the ground.

They thought he was dead. There seemed to be no breath in him. His head was bleeding from a cut, his hands bruised, his clothing torn. But fishermen have much experience in rescuing those whom the sea or the river have tried to claim, and they worked over the man, minute by minute. Although they could detect a faint motion of breathing, he would not return to life and consciousness.

They leaned back on their heels, shaking their heads, when a tremulous sigh pushed through the blue lips and the head moved. And they hurried back to their work of getting the lungs to empty themselves of the water, watching how breathing grew stronger and color came back into the deeply tanned face, and the eyes opened at last.

Louis Jolliet looked up into the concerned, sea-weathered, kindly faces of the two fishermen. Not far away he dimly heard the roaring of the rapids, and then memory flooded back. He tried to sit up but fell back in a weakness which angered him, and he tried again. A fisherman supported him, then, and Louis gasped a few words in a hoarse, waterlogged voice, spitting more water.

Where was the boy? Where was the canoe? The chest, the men? *Where was the boy?*

They did not know what he meant. They had seen nothing, no canoe, no men, no chest, certainly no boy. Louis put his head in his hands and groaned, and the tears which he would not have shed for the death of the men—for they were men, and part of their living was to die when God willed—he shed for the little Indian boy who was to have gone with him to Québec and, perhaps, to have been like a son to him. All gone. The papers, the map, all the fruits of the shining voyage of discovery. All were gone . . . and now as memory returned more strongly, he was thankful to God that he had left the copies of map and journal at the Sault.

When he could talk, he explained what had happened,

about the rapids, about the journey, that he was Jolliet come
back from the west and the Great River; but they had not
heard of him, or even of the Great River, wherever that was.
The only rivers they knew were the Ottawa, dastardly in its
rapids, and the St. Lawrence, taking their fishing boats out
to sea. But they were sad for his misfortune and for the
grief that made this strong dark man weep into his paddle-
creased fingers as he sat on the rock above the rapids.

12

~~~~~~

CLAIRE-FRANÇOISE

THE RETURN TO QUÉBEC was anything but triumphal. He had
not really expected that it would be. Men came back from
the distant wilderness every day and were noticed very little
by the public, which went about its usual business and let
them come and go as they willed.

But Louis Jolliet was back in town after having traveled
more than a thousand miles to the west. He had found an
unknown river and canoed 1,110 miles down its length, returning by way of another river which had tremendous
possibilities as a linking waterway for the glory of France
and the revenues of the King. And instead of coming home
with proof of these activities, he had returned in a wilder-
ness-worn, tattered suit of clothes, his disgraceful appearance being that of one who had been left in the water a
little too long. He had no proof of what he had done or
where he had been—at least not until he could go back to
the Sault and get his duplicate map and journal. He had lost
all the pelts in the river during the upset which had also
destroyed the canoe he was bringing back to Adrien's widow,
Jeanne. It was true that the voyage had not been kind to
the canoe; neither had the Quapaws. It had been sadly
worn and patched and was hardly worth bringing back, except that it had been a loan and he was obliged in honor

to return what he had borrowed. Besides, it had still been good enough to bring him to the forty-second rapid. It would be embarrassing to explain to Jeanne about this, as well as the loss of the pelts which had been rightfully hers.

He was deeply depressed when he started down the St. Lawrence and stopped at Cap-de-la-Madeleine to see Jeanne and her little boy, Adrien's son, to explain what had happened. He did not especially wish to see her husband, Antoine Baillargé, the drunkard and gambler.

But Antoine Baillargé was no longer among the living. He had died in December, 1672, after Louis had left for the west so that he had not known about it. Nor did he know that Jeanne had remarried not long afterward. Her husband was now Mathurin Normandin. Far from being reckless with money as Baillargé had been, Normandin, a thin-lipped, miserly sort, was very anxious to obtain everything that was rightfully his, and his wife's as well.

Normandin had a low opinion of Louis Jolliet, who had been away far too long from the family business to help it very much, and who was not noted, besides, for ever making any great profits. Nevertheless, since Louis had been given power of attorney when Adrien Jolliet went west on the fateful journey from which he had never returned, Normandin expected that his wife's property should have been better handled. That was the trouble when a man lived too long with the priests, and the rest of the time in the woods doing no one knew what. No business sense—but he, Normandin, would not stand for being bilked of his wife's just claims.

He greeted Louis with a little less than hospitality at the door of the house in Cap-de-la-Madeleine. He grudgingly let him in and, before he started to talk, permitted the delighted Jeanne to serve the returned explorer some soup and wine and thick bread with new butter.

The talk, once Mathurin Normandin commenced, sickened Louis. He was sick enough, inside, from what had happened, and this noisy Normandin irritated him so much that he put down his spoon and stood up, suddenly powerful and full of fury. Normandin left off haranguing him on his failure to make any profits out of the family business, let alone destroying the canoe Jeanne had lent him. Without saying anything to Jeanne who, wide-eyed and wordless, sadly watched him go, or to Normandin, who was left with his mouth open, Louis slammed out of the door and set off on foot back to Montréal. His fury carried him halfway to Trois Rivières before he knew where he was. Then he slowed down a trifle.

But Mathurin Normandin hadn't finished with his wife's former brother-in-law. He had papers served on Jolliet in Montréal, demanding full settlement for a long list of debts, including costs of some seventy pelts and the canoe that were lost in the rapids, as well as the forge at Sault Ste Marie, and various supplies, and literally the clothes on his back, dunning him for the old shirt, pants, and necktie of Adrien's which he evidently had borrowed or bought on credit from Jeanne when he went west the first time.

Louis had little or nothing with which to pay the claims. The suit, however, was settled with a compromise, the details of which are lacking. The result very likely did not please the irascible Normandin, but Louis was thankful to be quit of the matter, even if it left him penniless. The settlement was signed before Benigne Basset, the royal notary of Montréal.

Two months later, Jolliet was called before the Sovereign Council in another lawsuit involving the widow of François de Chavigny, one of the members of the company, who had died in 1673. His widow demanded Chavigny's share of the profits; his mother wanted a part, too. Louis was also summoned to give an account of his trading activities in the west, and to explain why he had in fact done so poorly. Then certain members of the expedition, who had evidently returned from the Sault—Plattier, Tiberge, Moreau, and Largilier—added their voices in demanding more than they had received from the meager profits of the expedition.

It had all become a maddening tangle of suits and counter-suits, which Frontenac and the Council finally ended briskly by sentencing everyone involved in the company to equal shares in the costs of bringing out the furs left at the Sault, as well as equal shares in the ultimate profits, if any.

Even before this second lawsuit took place, the next blow hit Louis when he was in Québec, shortly before August 1.

A ruinous fire had destroyed the mission at Sault Ste Marie. Nothing had been saved, not even the church chapel furnishings. The superior, Father Dablon, told Louis about it on the day when he came in to recount what he and Father Marquette had seen and done. Louis stopped, transfixed with dismay. Would disaster never end? In that mission at the Sault he had left the copies of his journal and map.

Now all of his records were lost. He did not know then that Father Marquette had, during the winter, completed a map of his own. He knew that the priest had made notes along the way, but many of them were not of the things which he, Jolliet, with careful calculation and study, had observed and written.

Laboriously, finally, he redrew his map for Frontenac. But Louis felt with dissatisfaction that his original map had been undoubtedly better and more accurate than all he might recall and put on paper now. Without either journal or map, he found that he had forgotten some of the small items, some of the locations in relation to each other. Yet slowly he worked, trying to recapture what had been lost.

Meanwhile, he had several long interviews with Father Dablon, who carefully wrote down all Jolliet could tell him. Later, Dablon combined Jolliet's verbal account with some of the details in Marquette's incomplete notes, and put in some of his own observations of Indians on Lake Michigan. The result of this carefully compiled account of the Jolliet-Marquette voyage has been called Marquette's Journal, but it was not that entirely. It was a composite, and in Claude Dablon's handwriting.

Dablon did what was expected of a superior before any of the Jesuit reports were sent to Paris for publication: he edited, compressed, where necessary he rewrote. But in the case of the 1673 expedition, Dablon found himself in the peculiar situation of having history-making material under his fingers. Here was history which had been made in part by one of his priests, one who was capable and intelligent enough to evaluate what he saw, but who certainly was not the leader of the expedition. Dablon knew this and so did Louis Jolliet; so did Talon and Frontenac. They had sent Jolliet, not Marquette, to find the Mississippi. But when Father Dablon wrote the journal which is purported to be Marquette's, sometimes using the latter's own words, sometimes his own, sometimes the things which Jolliet told him, he somehow conveyed the ultimate impression that it was Marquette's expedition and discoveries, and that it was the priest who was the leader. It was a natural thing for Dablon to do. Perhaps he did not realize the implications or historical confusion in what he did. He loved Father Marquette and knew that this journal would be his immortal epitaph.

On his own part, Louis Jolliet wrote to Frontenac about what he had seen and done, and what had happened. He also wrote to Bishop Laval, who was just then in France, and laid open far more of his inner feelings than he had in the more businesslike document to Frontenac, who was still virtually a stranger to him.

My Lord,

It is not long since I am back from my voyage to the Sea of the South. I was favored by good fortune during the whole time, but on my return, when I was about to reach Montréal, my canoe capsized and I lost two men and a box wherein were all my papers, my journal, as well as some curios from those far off countries. I am much grieved over the loss of a ten-year-old slave who had been presented to me. He was of a good disposition, quick-witted, diligent, and obedient. He could express himself in French, and was beginning to read and write. I lost consciousness, and after four hours in the water, I was found by fishermen who never go to this place and who would not have been there if the Blessed Virgin had not obtained for me this grace from God, Who stayed the course of nature in order to rescue me from death.

Except for this shipwreck, Your Excellency would have had a quite interesting relation, but all I saved is my life.

There is a bitter note in this laconic conclusion which expresses something of what the man was feeling. Both his courage and his spirits were at a low ebb. "All I saved is my life," he says, as if this were a minor matter now and that nothing really mattered; as if he were the least item of value left out of the water, saved, for what purpose? With almost all of his money paid to the rapacious Normandin and no more coming in until Zacharie arrived with the rest of the pelts from the Sault, and no great future ahead that he could see, Louis didn't know what would come next. He was obviously not only a poor businessman but an ineffectual explorer, as well.

He had received another blow on his return when he learned that his old friend, and his father's friend before that, François Bissot, had died during the summer. Louis went at once to call upon the widow and her family. Marie Bissot wept a bit on Louis's strong shoulder while he patted her gently and told her how grieved he was to learn of the good man's passing. François Bissot had in many ways taken Jean Jolliet's place in Louis's life, while Marie herself was almost as close to him as his own mother, at times even closer in understanding. The eleven Bissot children had been like members of his own family, though during the years in the seminary he had not seen very much of them.

François Bissot had been given fishing rights on Egg Island and along the north coast of the Gulf of St. Lawrence, and had done well in developing the fisheries and peltries of this long-neglected area. Marie each summer usually had gone with him out to the camp on Egg Island, and taken her growing family, ultimately all eleven of them, for a summer of work and frolic.

Granddaughter of Louis Hébert, Marie had become a woman of character who ruled her large family with a strong dominance tempered with love and laughter. When other Québec women stayed at home and worried about the whereabouts and lives of their fishing or trapping husbands and sons, Marie had chosen to go with François whenever it was possible.

Consequently, in Louis's years at the seminary, he himself was too much engrossed in his studies to see much of his friends or relatives during the winter months, and in summer when he sometimes had a holiday, the Bissots were away on Egg Island.

But after he left the seminary he was in Québec during the winters and got into the habit of spending many of the snow-banked evenings in the warm, laughter-filled Bissot house which always seemed overflowing with children, dogs, a couple of cats, and, of late, a growing assortment of grandchildren. Even before he went to the Mississippi, therefore, he had begun to focus his attention on one of the Bissot girls. They were all pretty and high-spirited and intelligent, but now one of them seemed to stand out from the others.

Claire-Françoise Bissot must have been typical of many of the Canadian girls—small-boned, dark-eyed and dark-haired, with well-defined black eyebrows and long lashes, and the clear, rosy complexion which a northern atmosphere bequeathed its people. When Louis went away on the expedition, he not only went to say good-by to his mother and his aunts, his sister, and Mme Bissot and her flock, but to bid farewell to burly François, too, who had kissed him heartily and wished him a God's blessing on the project. He had also gone specifically to say good-by to Claire-Françoise. He remembered afterward that her eyes had been full of tears when she stood in the doorway to wave to him as he went.

And on the long journey, now and again, her lovely, serious, wistful face at his leave-taking had come back to his memory, so that in spirit she had traveled with him down the rivers and back. But when he had gone to see her on his return, it was not now to see her alone, but to mourn with Marie Bissot on their mutual loss in François's passing. The old house seemed curiously empty and echoing without his big laugh and his stomping about when he was excited, and the songs he sometimes had suddenly burst into singing in an off-key bass which shook the holy figures on the family altar.

All that winter in Québec, when the snows were drifted high along the streets, with only a track for sledges to get through, and the river again was a mass of immobile ice, Louis went to visit with Marie Bissot, and with Claire-Françoise.

His courting was not a rapid thing. By the time spring

came and the wild plums sent a delirious fragrance into the warming air, the two went for long walks along the ramparts and talked of what they would do in the years when they would always be together. Without really knowing how it had come about, Louis and Claire found themselves pledged to be married in the fall. He would like to wait until then when members of his family had come back from the Sault and the sea, and when he himself had put by a little money. Claire was willing to wait.

At thirty years of age, Louis Jolliet knew that he had found what he should have known years before: the woman who would make his life complete was Claire-Françoise. She was nineteen, and she, too, had been in no hurry to marry, though there were plenty of young men, and widowers, too, who were eager for the chance. She had waited for Louis, and he had certainly taken his time about it, her mother had occasionally muttered in exasperation.

In a way, it was unusual for two people like this handsome, strong, intelligent pair to have waited so long for marriage. Though the King some time before had put a fatherly yet stern decree upon the unmarried ones in Québec, insisting that the men be wed by the time they were twenty, and the girls by sixteen, with stiff fines for failure in this respect, and nice bonuses bestowed on big families, the King seemed strangely to have ignored these two. Both were certainly well past the decreed marriageable age, and were almost elderly by Québec standards.

On October 1, 1675, a marriage contract was drawn up. It was witnessed and signed by a remarkable gathering of people. One, of course, was Marie Couillard Bissot, who, only three weeks before, at the advanced age of forty-two, had married Jacques Lalande, who was twenty-seven. Another name on the contract was Guillaumette Hébert Couillard, Claire's grandmother, and daughter of the revered

Louis Hébert. There was Denis Joseph Ruette d'Auteuil, procurer-general of Québec, the husband of Claire's godmother, who was also there. Geneviève Macart, first cousin of the bride-to-be and the wife of the eminent Charles Bazier, receiver-general, also signed. So did Louise and Marie Bissot, Claire's sisters, and Éstienne Charet, Marie Bissot's husband; and Jacques Leber, prominent merchant of Montréal, Jolliet's good friend; and Louis Rouer de Villeray, first counselor of the King in the Sovereign Council. They were important and vivid people. But one name was lacking.

Marie d'Abancourt Jolliet Guillot Prévost, though she was one of the gathering fondly come to witness her son's marriage contract, did not sign. Of all that group, Marie d'Abancourt could not write her name. Although Guillaumette Hébert Couillard was older, she could inscribe hers very well indeed, with considerable style, but Marie lacked this ability for a simple enough reason. Guillaumette Hébert had been born in France in the year 1606 and had come to Québec with her parents in 1617. Thus she had had time to be educated in one of the excellent convent schools in Paris, and so could read and write and cipher very well. But Marie d'Abancourt, born in France in 1618, had come to Québec when she was very young, at a time when there was no education available for girls in the colony. And so little Marie grew up without formal learning, which was considered of no great handicap in that time or place. Happily illiterate and entirely self-sufficient, she was descended from the illustrious Chevalier Adrien d'Abancourt whose family in 1455 had known wealth and high position in France. But in Québec, on an October day in 1675, when she could not sign her name on her famous son's marriage contract, perhaps Marie d'Abancourt knew secret shame.

Everyone represented in that contract had, each in his own way, before, now, or later, played or would play a part in the life of Louis Jolliet. The document shows these splendidly virile and interesting signatures, with those of Louis and Claire at the top.

It was on a Tuesday that the contract was signed, and the wedding took place on the next Monday, in the Cathedral of Québec. The party gathered in the Bissot house in the upper town, where Claire-Françoise, with a great to-do, was being dressed by all her sisters, her mother supervising the procedure. Two of the younger children had gone out to the marshes to gather the last of the blue gentians, spared by frost, for garden flowers had been ruined a week before. Claire must have a bouquet! Her white muslin gown, which she herself had made, with its full skirts and lace inserts and collar, was charming. Her cheeks were flushed with excitement as her mother adjusted the veil over the crisp black hair, kissed her and blessed her, and wept a moment. The bride was ready.

They walked to the church, the whole large family and kinfolk and friends, with all the Jolliets and even Jeanne Normandin, Adrien's widow, coming in from Cap-de-la-Madeleine for the affair.

The throng filled the cathedral. A hush fell as the acolytes lighted the altar candles; there was a settling back in peace as the organ music began to swell forth.

Father Henri de Bernières, vicar-general of the Bishop of Québec, parish priest of the Cathedral, entered the church, and the marriage service began. Louis would have liked having Bishop Laval himself perform the ceremony, but Laval was still away in France.

In a small house in the lower town of Québec, Louis and Claire-Françoise set up their new home. He knew that he must now settle down to making a living—a reliable living to support a family. He became a merchant in Québec, handling the family business there, while Zacharie and the others in the old company still operated the warehouse at the Sault. There is no record that Louis Jolliet ever went out there again.

He was settled and content with home and wife and business, and he became the regular organist at the cathedral. But as spring came and the geese went north again to the tundra around Hudson Bay, and the Indians came down from the lakes with furs, he found himself growing more and more restive, and Claire-Françoise, who had known how her father was in spring, may have worried a little. She was expecting her child in summer and did not want her husband to go away just then.

Louis went to Trois Rivières when the Indians began coming that spring. He questioned some of them. Far fewer canoes and pelts had come down from the wilderness this year, and he wondered, as many an official and fur man wondered, if the English were in fact waylaying the Indians and giving better prices, as they had been rumored to be doing. Perhaps it was the illegal *coureurs des bois* who were still getting away with far more than anyone suspected, thus draining away from the St. Lawrence the flood of furs which should have been coming.

Nevertheless, simply the presence of the sleek Indian canoes on the river, scattered though they were that year and hurtful to his business, to Louis were a sign that spring had come back to the upper country. But he went back to Québec and his work.

The baby was born on August 11, 1676, in Québec. They named the boy Louis, for his father and for the King.

And with the child safely born and things going well at home, and with his business prospering moderately, Louis Jolliet grew more and more impatient with city life. The west forever called. Over and over again, when he lay awake at night beside the sleeping Claire, or when, with a far look in his eyes, he gazed out of the window or across the St. Lawrence, and thought of another river, the most beautiful he had ever seen, he yearned to go back to the country of the Illinois. He would take his wife and son and a small company of men, to settle there as a part of New France, a veritable Eden-corner of the New World.

When he could stand it no longer, he talked to M. Duchesneau, the intendant, about it, and the intendant promised to bring up the matter with Colbert, the colonial minister, in his next letter to France. Duchesneau liked Jolliet. He would do his best for him. The letter went on the last boat before winter closed the harbor and the snows resumed with a vast white finality. Louis had to wait all through the winter to know what the answer would be.

The first ship back in the harbor in the spring of 1677 brought a letter from Colbert. It was terse, and it held devastating negation for Louis Jolliet.

His Majesty is unwilling to grant the leave asked by the Sieur Jolliet to go to the Illinois Country with twenty men in order to begin a settlement there. The number of settlers in Canada should be increased before thinking of settlements elsewhere; this should be your guiding principle in regard to newly made discoveries.

The intendant regretfully relayed the message to Jolliet. And the beautiful, the alluring, the kindly Illinois country was lost to him. No man could go there without the King's consent, not unless he were an outlaw defying the mandates of the colony.

It was a bitter dose to swallow, and the dreams which he had allowed himself to hold like a shining globe all during the snowstorms and bright dazzle of winter sunshine, all through the glittering, star-filled nights when the northern lights lit the heavens with the glory of God, vanished in defeat.

He felt even more bitter the following year when he learned that the fickle King had actually granted to that blowhard, La Salle, who was always promising big things but seldom got around to accomplishing them, much the same thing which Jolliet had been refused. In 1678, La Salle was given land along the Illinois River where he was to build a fort and ships, start a colony, and pave the way for France's traffic and dominion between the lakes and the Gulf of Mexico. This was the same plan which Jolliet had had years earlier—his colony, his waterway, his canal, his country. But it was not for him now.

La Salle, incompetent to handle such a venture, failed and failed again. Jolliet, angered by the ruination of a project which he felt that he himself might have carried off more successfully, watched as La Salle blundered, knew mutiny, Indian attack, failure, while the lovely Illinois country waited in vain for Louis Jolliet to return.

The same springtime which brought the ship bearing news of his refusal also brought canoes down from the lakes bearing messages from the missions. It was then that Louis learned that his dear friend, Jacques Marquette, had been one to be permitted to go back to preach in the Illinois country. Ill but full of transcendent determination, he dwelt with the Indians throughout the dreadful winter, battling a disease which was wasting him. Trying to get back to the mission at Green Bay in spring, he and the two Frenchmen and his Indian companions were forced to land near what is now Ludington, Michigan.

They made him as comfortable as they could—the sorrowing Indians and the faithful Pierre Moreau and Jacques Largilier, two of the men from the 1673 expedition who had gone back there. Marquette gave them careful instructions regarding the prayers for the dying and for his funeral. Then the priest died. He had had his most deeply cherished wish—to serve the people of the Illinois country, and to die there, and be buried near the lake he loved, Lake Michigan.

Louis, hearing the news, felt both sad and happy. He was grieved that the priest no longer lived, but he was happy that he had had his wish. Only Louis Jolliet, it seemed, was not permitted to go out to the west again.

13

~~~~~~

THE NORTHWARD TRAIL

WHEN HE MIGHT HAVE TAKEN MATTERS into his own hands
and gone off to the west without permission, the sudden
chance for adventure of which he had never dreamed lay
open to him.

Since the refusal of his plan to set a colony along the
Illinois River, he had been very busy at home. Madeleine
Macart sold him a house she owned in the lower town of
Québec. It was situated on the Rue Sous le Fort, at the
bottom of Mountain Hill, almost directly below the cliff
where Frontenac lived in the upper town, in the elegant
Chateau St. Louis.

The Jolliets were settled in the new house in time for
their second child, Charles, to be born there on June 18,
1678. There was even more need now for the larger home,
for the younger brothers and sisters of Claire-Françoise
also lived with them. So did Marie Bissot and her new
husband, Lalande. Louis, disliking the untaught crudeness
and obvious lack of education in the young Bissots, and
not being able to afford to send them all to the Ursulines
or the Jesuits, set himself, during the winter, to giving them
lessons. It renewed some of the things in his mind which
he had almost forgotten and gave him a pleasure in teaching.

Inextricably bound with family partnerships, into which

he seemed to get himself ever deeper, he renewed his business contract with Jacques Lalande in the downriver fisheries. He hired a shoemaker for a year to make up a supply of footwear for his large and growing family, and he sold to his brother Zacharie, now back in Québec, a share in the ship which he bought in 1676 from Michel le Neuf de la Vallière.

But between his labors in the fisheries and the seal-oil business, he worked nights on revising the nomenclature of his map of the Mississippi. He had slowly and carefully redrawn it to replace the one claimed by the rapids. On the first one he had called the great river "Rivière du Buade," in honor of Frontenac's family name, but he felt that now, perhaps after Frontenac's rebuff, it would be more properly called "Rivière de Messisipi." "Lac Frontenac" he changed to "Lac Ontario," its Indian name. He decided that this was more fitting and enduring than to play the fleeting game of politics and name these timeless landmarks for someone who, a generation hence, might be discredited or forgotten.

Frontenac was just now a powerful man, it was true, though not at first especially cordial to Jolliet. Frontenac had tremendously impressed the Iroquois by making a great show of building a fort at Cataraqui on Lake Ontario, erecting it with great speed and drama under the astonished eyes of the awed Iroquois who had gathered to hear what the great Onontio had to say to them, and who stayed to watch the fort go up in a day. Frontenac knew how to cajole, overpower, and impress the sensibilities of the Indians, not only by what he did, but by his own tremendous confidence in himself. He expected them to be awed by him, and they were.

But in his own private business dealings, he was obviously, to those who knew the inside of things, trafficking with the illegal *coureurs des bois* in the illicit fur business, and was carrying on many hidden deceits. A man had to augment the poor pay the King gave governors, Frontenac argued. He could neatly manage the Iroquois with one hand and rake in profits with the other. The more Louis Jolliet learned of this man, the less he wished to perpetuate his name profusely on the new map. He did, however, decide to leave the name of Fort Frontenac; this was really an admirable accomplishment of the governor's, but lake and river should bear the more dignified and longer-lasting, truly American names with which they had been originally endowed.

It was through Duchesneau, not Frontenac, that Jolliet was at last given a small recognition for his work in the west. In 1679 he was granted jointly, together with Jacques de Lalande, all the "isles and islets called Mingan, situated along the northern bank of the St. Lawrence down the bay named Lance aux Espagnols" [Brador Bay].

This concession, a splendid one, gave them leave to establish cod and seal fisheries everywhere on the islands and shores of this vast stretch of the north coast of the Gulf of St. Lawrence. This was some of the richest fishing territory in all of New France. The Mingan concession was just the beginning of a belated public awakening to Jolliet's merits.

But Louis Jolliet still pondered the unsolved riddle of the north. The northern mystery extended not only along the Mississippi and to the possible route to the Pacific, but directly north, to the controversial area of Hudson Bay. Virtually unknown, lying cold and remote and mysterious far above Québec and the St. Lawrence, it had become a point of bitter controversy between the English and the French. Both wanted it. Both claimed to have got there first and so, by right of conquest, it belonged to England, one said, or to France, the other insisted. The main difficulty, however, was not so much that either nation really wanted this uncomfortable and long-frozen Arctic stretch of the American continent, but that they felt it might lead to the way to the Pacific. More practically and immediately, each coveted the northern trading rights.

The English traders enticed the Indians to bring their pelts to trading posts on the Rupert River and along the south shore of Hudson Bay, while the French, waiting in mounting fury and frustration down at Tadoussac and Trois Rivières for Indians who never came, had fewer and fewer profits.

Where once the Company of One Hundred Associates had known great wealth from furs brought to the annual trade fairs along the St. Lawrence, failure now seemed imminent. It was all the fault of the English, they complained bitterly, but, in the main, a large part of this trouble was due to a pair of French traitors who evidently did not know which side to stay on. The Sieur des Groseilliers and the Sieur Radisson, brothers-in-law, had been exploring around the north for years, had claimed to have seen the upper Mississippi long before any other white man got around to mentioning it, were always appearing and disappearing at unlikely times and places, and then showing up with improbable tales of their adventurings.

When they, by design, helped the English beat the French out of a good many thousands of francs worth of trade, they were considered to be treasonable villains by France and Canada. Therefore, they blandly went over to the English to work for them. It was the amiable Des Groseilliers and Radisson who were largely responsible, at least the French thought—it was convenient to blame anyone who was handy, and these two were—for tolling the Indians and their pelts away from French trading posts and leading them to the English.

In 1672 when Frontenac came to Québec, and discovered what was going on up there, he made hasty plans and wrote to Colbert lengthily. He added this postscript:

> I forgot to inform you, my Lord, that upon learning that Des Groseilliers was enticing all the Indians away from us and by making them presents was attracting them to Hudson Bay, where he has an establishment, I determined to make use of the zeal of Father Albanel, Jesuit, who wished to go and open a mission in that part of the country. He will endeavor to dissuade the Indians, with whom he has great influence, from going thither. The said Father Albanel will sound out Des Groseilliers, if he encounter him, and will try to win him over to our side.

But Father Albanel, with an excess of poor judgment which almost cost him his life, left Québec too late in the season and had to spend a wild and bitter winter in the wastes of upper Canada. Finally, after a desperate journey, he reached Hudson Bay in September, 1672.

Father Albanel had indeed blazed a trail to Hudson Bay, but while there he was detained by the English governor, Charles Bayly, who summarily shipped him off to England in 1673, and that was that. Father Albanel had no opportunity to exert any influence on anyone, neither the Indians nor the miscreant renegades.

At Québec, Duchesneau was growing increasingly uneasy about the situation on the mysterious northern bay, which had access from the sea so that any ship from England could slip in and out at will, and the French would not know about it. He wished he could send a reliable person, one not likely to be seduced by the English nor intimidated by the governor; preferably one who was expert in traveling in the northern wilderness, and who could map an overland route.

He sent for Louis Jolliet.

The request to go to Hudson Bay came in 1679 when he

had just settled the rights of fishing along the north coast
of the St. Lawrence, had been cod-fishing off the bleak
shores of Egg Island and the Seven Islands. He had taken
seals and had directed his Indians in rendering out the oil,
to be brought back in casks. He was prospering at last,
though it often seemed that after his associates had their
share, there was not a great surplus for him. He might never
grow rich, but at least he was making a good living for his
family. At the same time, he disliked the mounting sameness in his life. To a man who had adventure in his blood
and couldn't stay in one place very long at a time without
sniffing the air for what lay beyond the next hill, the business of catching fish and rendering out seal oil could grow
monotonous.

And now once again adventure opened. He left the fisheries in care of some of his trusted men, and took with him
seven others. Zacharie Jolliet went along this time, for Zacharie had probably reproached Louis a good many times for
leaving him at the Sault when he and the others went off
down the Mississippi. So Zacharie went, and so did Claire-
Françoise's brother, Guillaume Bissot, as well as the Lesart
brothers, Étienne and Pierre, and the Le Mieux brothers,
Louys and Pierre, and a man whose name appeared in the
account only as Denys.

The plan was to visit rivers and lakes which lay within
the territory of the trading area of Tadoussac, and find out
what was happening there and what the English were doing
on Hudson Bay. It was a monumental job when the scope of
the vast subarctic territory was considered, but neither
Duchesneau nor Jolliet realized this at the time.

In three canoes the party set off on May 13, 1679. Louis
may have remembered that it was almost on that very same
date six years earlier that he and Jacques Marquette had
departed from the mission at St. Ignace de Michilimackinac

to find the great river. They had been six memorable years marked by the arrival of his two cherished sons. A third child was expected that very autumn. He assured Claire-Françoise that he would surely be back before the baby was born.

Now on a fine May day, Louis and his men departed early and paddled down the St. Lawrence to the place where great brooding dark cliffs, like portals of a giant's doorway, opened into the clear, cold, dark waters of the Saguenay, and turned the canoes up into its silence, to no one knew what goal.

14

~~~~~~

HUDSON BAY

DAY AFTER DAY they traversed the difficulties and the magnificence of the wild Saguenay with its mountainous rim covered with sparse trees and purple-gray rocks, the dark spruce forests massed in more sheltered places. The spruces grew lower and more wind-battered as the way was ever more northward. Then the river became narrower, the cliffs less precipitous, and finally the river wound in rambling fashion through low, rocky, moss-covered, flower-strewn muskeg and tundra, stretching almost level to the horizon.

The marshy pools were full of ducks. Geese and plovers and sandpipers had their eggs in tundra hollows, bedded on the cold moss and lichen. As the canoes passed there was a disturbance among the nesting birds—the air suddenly full of wings and wild cries, subsiding again as soon as they had passed.

Laboriously, the canoes continued on their tedious way. There were so many detours and so many portages that, on the entire trip, they traveled more than twice the distance that geese flying to their nesting grounds would have. But they were men in frail canoes; and therefore, they had to make no fewer than 127 portages, some long and some short, between Tadoussac and Hudson Bay.

In all this wild muskeg country they saw very few Indians

143

and learned nothing from the few they did find. They passed from the Saguenay eventually, into the still mirrorings of Lake Mistassini by way of the Peribonka and the Temiscaming, left the lake via the Marten River which, with a great deal of winding, beaver dams, and portages, got them to Lake Nemiskau and into the Rupert River.

At last on a chill, bright, windy day they were paddling up the widening Rupert when they came to a cape thrusting ahead of them and hiding the view beyond. Tidal deposits along the mud shore, as well as a smell of the sea in the wind, had convinced Jolliet that they must now be close to Hudson Bay. As they rounded the cape, he saw it at last— James Bay, that southern embayment of the greater Hudson Bay, lying ahead. It spread lovely and calm and blue under the summer sky, a great expanse of pale water with what he decided in excitement might be an iceberg standing white against the horizon. But closer in focus was something else of far more immediate importance to Louis Jolliet and his men.

An English fort stood only a scant league away on the south bank of the Rupert River.

The tide was going out. It drew the canoes inexorably down the river without their having to be paddled until they were soon almost abreast of the fort. Everything was very quiet. There lay over shore and fort and river and bay a dreamlike calm, punctuated by bird calls, as if this were all unreal and no life but their own were here. But Louis knew that this was no dream. This was the stronghold of the enemy, the English, and he didn't want some sudden sentry popping out and discovering them. He might lose his wits and send a charge of cannon into the canoes.

Louis loaded his pistol and fired a shot into the air. The noise resounded and echoed against a nothingness of silence; it startled the terns and jaegers flying past, so that they

veered with a shrill cackling and commotion. A crowd of
agitated plovers rose from the nearby tundra and flew in
circles, squeaking and piping in alarm.

No one came out of the fort. Instead, on the opposite
bank of the river, to which the French had had their backs
all this time and could, they realized with an immediate
shudder of apprehension, have been picked off easily between the shoulders by any fair marksman, there suddenly
appeared three Englishmen. They were out hunting. Their
boat was beached because the tide was out; they were in
fact stranded opposite the fort until the tide came in and
floated the boat so they could cross.

From the distance, the hunters evidently took the Frenchmen in their deerskin clothes, and their swarthy, sunbrowned
complexions and dark hair, to be Indians come to trade, so
they shouted cheerfully in some Indian tongue for them to
come on over and get them, the English, and take them to
the fort where they could all do business.

Jolliet directed his men to paddle cautiously over to the
far shore so the English could see who they were. He still
didn't want the hunters to be too much surprised, with unfortunate results for the visitors.

The three Englishmen came trotting across the springy
muskeg, sloshing their way as they talked, while Jolliet and
the others sat in the canoes, fought mosquitoes and black
flies, and waited to be seen more clearly. Then Jolliet called
out a greeting in French, and the man in the lead stopped
as if shot. He had such an amazed and disconcerted expression that Jolliet began to laugh, and the others joined him.

The Englishman whirled about and dashed back as fast
as he could to his companions, who were some three hundred paces behind. Louis called cajolingly to have no fear—
that they were friends. They saw him rejoin his companions
and explain, with much gesturing and many fearful glances

cast back over his shoulder at the men in the three canoes, which were again drifting with the tide. The three Englishmen refused to come any closer, but stood where they were and stared, shielding their eyes with their hands against the brilliant arctic light.

Louis decided that the ridiculous situation had gone far enough. He and his men got out on shore and walked quietly toward the English, who looked ready to flee if they came too close. Jolliet spoke to them in French, and there was one man who, fortunately, knew a smattering of the language, and at least caught on to what was happening. In halting, crude French, he asked who they were.

"I am a Frenchman," Louis called out pleasantly, "and my name is Jolliet."

The man came closer. He was still fearful. After a certain amount of reassuring conversation and much gesturing, the Englishmen were convinced of the visitors' harmlessness.

Meanwhile a fourth Englishman, who had been farther off and who had seen all that happened, came up and joined them. He was inordinately amused at the scant show of bravery in his countrymen, and was filled with so much glee over the matter that he made fun of them all the way back to the fort. This delighted the French, who, though they might not exactly understand what was being said, could guess enough of it, and from the discomfited and embarrassed expressions of the timid ones, could surmise the roasting they were getting.

The man sharing Louis's canoe on the way to the other shore could not understand French at all, so Louis tried Latin, and was pleased to find that this man, far up here in the remote Hudson Bay country, knew Latin well enough to carry on a conversation in it. While the canoes were paddled across the sluggish Rupert River, with the pale waters of Hudson Bay beyond and the icebergs standing in the far distance, the two talked in measured Latin sentences, explaining everything.

But not too much. Louis himself left much unsaid. He didn't want the English to think the French were spying, which was, of course, exactly what they were doing.

The Latin-speaking man pointed out the peninsula where the governor lived, while a ship with twelve guns was anchored in the bay nearby, and two smaller vessels were not far away. Landing on the muddy tidal shore, the French were escorted in great hospitality to the fort and were given food. Not very good food because, it was explained, provisions were scant, and daily the English at the fort were looking for the ship from England due with supplies. If it did not come soon, they should have to rely on hunting and fishing for their food. They would need ammunition soon, also, and a good deal else in order to last out the winter.

Louis did not intend to stay here long. He had gained much that he wanted to see, but sociability with the lonely Englishmen at this forsaken arctic fort at the end of the world itself was not in his plans. He did not intend to wait to see the governor. The men at the fort, however, insisted that the governor would be deeply hurt if he did not see him. A man set out at once in a canoe to inform the governor that he had guests. Jolliet wrote a polite letter which he sent along with the messenger.

Sir:

Having been engaged by my Lord the Count of Frontenac, governor of all Canada, to visit the tribes and lands of the King's Domain in this part of the country, I came down as far as Lake Nemiskau intending to return by way of Three Rivers. When we reached Nemiskau our provisions were exhausted and we could find no game of any kind. The thought then came to me that in recent years several Frenchmen who had visited you returned with nothing but praise for the hearty welcome which you had accorded them, and I thought that you would be no less kind toward me than you had been toward them, and that you would be willing to sell me some hardtack and drink to facilitate my return. Your people give me hopes that you will come here. I shall not leave until tomorrow. If I am so fortunate as to see you, I shall be very glad to pay you my respects and to assure you that I am, etc. . . . .

This letter was a masterpiece of diplomacy and double talk, because, far from having ventured here just to get supplies, Jolliet had come to Hudson Bay for the specific reason of scouting out what was happening in this particular corner of the north. As for the "hearty welcome" which Bayly had given other French visitors, Jolliet had only to recall Father Albanel's treatment to realize the real danger in which he might find himself.

The governor was apparently delighted to have guests. It wasn't often he had the civilized sort, only Indians, except when the annual ship from England came.

Governor Bayly set off at once with fifteen men in a bark, but the wind disconcertingly failed them when they were halfway to the fort, and there they stuck, becalmed in the river. The governor and five sailors thereupon got into a dory, and the governor was rowed the rest of the way. Jolliet went to meet them, picking his way over the gray rocks and reindeer lichen, to avoid the mud of the shore.

But the governor couldn't reach the spot at which he wished to land. A sand bar prevented his coming ashore where Jolliet stood, and the dory swept by. The governor waved pleasantly with one hand, while he held securely to the gunwale with the other.

"Sir, I'll be with you in a moment," he called with impeccable British calm, and Jolliet wanted to laugh at the man's aplomb in this absurd situation.

At last the imperturbable governor found a suitable spot on which to land, and then came alone toward the waiting Jolliet. Four men stayed in the dory, while the fifth stood on shore with a musket in his hands. For all his cordiality, it was plain that the governor was no fool, and he was not going to be taken in by any false geniality on the part of his guests.

The two exchanged polite greetings. The governor said, as Jolliet later reported to Frontenac: "You are welcome, sir; you came here with peaceful intentions and you have nothing to fear. Stay as long as you like, and when you are ready to leave, I shall give you all the help I can for your return journey. I heard about you long ago," he went on, beaming at Jolliet, "and I am delighted to have the opportunity of talking to you and of hearing what you have to say about the great discovery of the river which the Indians call Mississippi, which flows in the direction of Mexico."

Then he added significantly: "The English think highly of discoverers."

The very friendliness of the English governor had a disarming quality, like a dog licking his fingers, and Jolliet may have felt some inner qualms of conscience at his own deception in coming here. The governor, in a guileless gesture of affection, took Jolliet by the hand and said: "Now come along. Since you have no intention of harming us, you certainly have no reason to fear that any harm will be done to you. Let us be friends!"

He signaled to his men to be on their way, and the wary-eyed soldier with the gun, dubiously watching what went on, reluctantly put down his musket and, with backward looks of distrust, returned to the dory, and they rowed down the river.

The two went to the fort. It was a barren and meager enough place, but it was all the hospitality which the cordial governor could provide. While Zacharie and the others were entertained by the soldiers, Governor Bayly and Jolliet seated themselves in a smaller room and talked. Bayly confessed to Louis that he was growing uneasy over the failure of his ship to return. So many things could have happened to prevent its arrival, and if it delayed much longer it could not get out again. He feared that ice in Davis Strait had already begun to form, or that drifting icebergs had wrecked the vessel, or that it had been waylaid somewhere by enemies. He was too polite to mention the French as the possible enemies, but Louis knew the thought was in his mind, as it was in his own; yet he did not feel that relations between France and England had reached such a pass that a supply ship bound for Hudson Bay's isolated post had been taken by the French.

Without committing himself too much, he tried to reassure Bayly, and the latter smiled, and apologized for his concern. He said it was a strange place for a man to be marooned; the very strangeness of the tundra and the muskeg, the loneliness, the great cold sea, the eerie icebergs, the implacable wilderness, all conspired to wreck a man's morale. He pointed out the curious white glimmer in the sky, low over the northern horizon, the iceblink reflected from ice fields even farther north.

Reduced though his supplies were, the governor still had a fine bottle of Madeira put by. He clapped his hands to summon an orderly, but none came. There was not a soul in the fort; the men were in their own quarters, entertaining the Frenchmen in Jolliet's party. The governor, remembering, smiled in apology and excused himself while he went to fetch the wine himself. He came back with two delicate crystal wine glasses which seemed totally out of place in this barren, silent, forsaken fort with the iceblink in the distant sky, and the tundra and the sea filling the whole world. A white whale splashed in the bay. But all of civilization and comfort were contained in the wicker-covered wine bottle and in the sparkling wine as it went into the glasses. The two men lifted them in a mutual toast to each other's success.

They sat over the wine all the rest of the afternoon, talking. Just the pleasure of conversing with an educated man—the governor evidently could speak French well—did Bayly a great deal of good, while Louis, who always enjoyed conversation, relished the situation to the full. He also learned a great many of the things which he had come here to find out, with no real prying, no spying, only listening to the garrulous governor.

He learned that the English had a ship of twelve guns patrolling the coast, the same vessel which he had seen riding at anchor when he came, and learned that the ice of last spring, when it broke up in bay and river, in great crushing floes and grinding masses, had splintered a forty-ton ship; but that Bayly had still another of the same tonnage, and another of fifteen tons, as well as three launches. It sounded very much as if the fort on Hudson Bay was well protected; that is, Louis reasoned, if the governor was really telling the truth and not bragging a bit. The only ship in sight was the twelve-gun bark in the bay.

But the others were used in trading along the rivers of the bay region, the governor said, down which the Indians came with their beaver pelts. And, Louis also learned with considerable interest, slowly sipping his wine and leaning comfortably back in his chair—a chair was certainly a relief after weeks in a canoe—that there were three other forts at quite a distance from one another, and that the English were making ready to build another one next spring.

He listened. He put in pleasant comments now and again, and quietly retained all that he heard. He learned that the

English were pushing more and more toward the west, toward the mouths of the rivers which had their headwaters
near Lake Superior, where many Indians lived who had for
a long time traded with the French.

The governor confirmed Jolliet's information, gleaned
from the few Indians he had met along the way, that the
English had been getting as many pelts as they wanted,
especially all the past year, ever since they had begun their
push toward the western rivers. This correspondingly marked
the leanest year at Tadoussac and Trois Rivières, and it all
fell into place, now, as Jolliet listened.

The governor was being very obliging in telling him what
he wanted to know, when Louis Jolliet's curiosity was suddenly piqued by something Bayly said. There was a gay
taunting light in the Englishman's pale eyes as he assured
his guest that even though the beaver trade had been very
good the past year and promised to be even better later on,
there was something else, something very much better, which
would make the Hudson Bay colony still more important in
the future. He stopped there, and poured some more wine.

Louis prodded him. He had quit too soon. What was this
"something better" which Bayly had mentioned? He was
curious; he always hated to be left in the dark on a mystery.
Just what . . . But Governor Bayly shook his head and
smiled pleasantly, if somewhat roguishly, and would not tell.
The coy secrecy worried Louis. If it was something which
Frontenac and Duchesneau ought to know about . . . but
the governor would not talk.

At least not about that. He went on further. Bayly had
taken a great liking to Louis Jolliet, as most people did after
they had begun to know him. He apparently had the kind of
personality which drew people to him, even the enemy,
which Bayly actually was, but even so the governor's proposition was astounding. For one of the reserved English, who

was busily knocking the economic props out from under the French, this plan was dumfounding to Louis.

To Governor Bayly it was not at all surprising, but only reasonable. Across the splintery table from him, opposite the delicate crystal wine glasses catching light in their liquid from the pale arctic sunshine, sat the foremost explorer of America, Louis Jolliet. He was indeed well known to the English, who admired and revered explorers. He was an expert mapmaker. He knew how to get on with Indians. Indians, in fact, liked him, and that spoke well for Jolliet. So it was to take advantage of the fact that he had here with him a noted hydrographer, well fitted mentally and physically to explore wilderness and evaluate his findings, that he propounded his invitation.

"If you will become my associate, Sieur Jolliet," proposed Bayly, suddenly serious, "I will pay you a lump sum of ten thousand francs and a salary of one thousand francs a year. I need to have someone like you to explore the country beyond the Assiniboin and establish a post among those Indians—" and they were the very Indians who had been coming down to do business with the French at Trois Rivières and Tadoussac for years, Louis knew.

Louis Jolliet smiled and shook his head. This was preposterous. He should have felt insulted, except that the governor seemed so innocent about his proposal. To ask him to become a traitor to king and country, like any Radisson and Des Groseilliers—to ask such a thing of him, Jolliet . . . he felt an anger rising hotly in him at the man's consummate audacity, then let himself cool. Obviously, Bayly was simply trying to take advantage of what he had at hand, and he needed a man like Jolliet. Not knowing how loyal he was, he took the opportunity to find out.

Jolliet gave himself time to control his anger before he answered. He knew that Bayly had it in his power to hold him here against his will, as he had held Father Albanel. There was no doubt, too, but that the money he offered would be excellent and a great deal more than he was able to earn in the fisheries or from the penny-pinching King of France, but there was still a matter of loyalty. Louis Jolliet was a proud man. He was not for sale.

He thanked the governor. He told Bayly firmly that he was a loyal Frenchman and always would be, that he gloried in serving the King, but it was indeed very kind of the governor to think of him. . . .

The governor pursued the matter, thinking he could change Jolliet's mind, thinking that perhaps the latter only played for time, bargaining for more money than had been offered. He really was worth more. It would be worth almost any amount to get this invaluable man into the service of England. France did not know the worth of what it had; doubtlessly underpaid him, too.

"The people of the Assiniboin," went on the governor thoughtfully, as if Jolliet had not given him a negative answer, and glancing up now and again at the listening visitor, whose mouth was still a little tight from his recent anger at being thought an easy man to be bought, "these people have the finest beaver pelts in all America. We know this, and so do you, Sieur Jolliet; and what have you French done to draw these excellent furs your way? Nothing, really, while we have sent presents to the Indians so that they may be favorably inclined to trade with us. We do not require them to come long distances with their pelts, as you do. We come to them in our ships, and they like this, for Indians are lazy. So there is no doubt, sir, that if the English remain in this bay, they will have control of all the commerce of Canada in ten years' time. You no doubt noted, down at Montréal, that the people of the Temiscaming and those of

Routin's band did not come there last year. We came to them, instead.

"Besides," Bayly concluded as a clincher, "they found that by coming down the Moose River the way was shorter, and we paid them two, three, even four times more for their pelts than you did on the St. Lawrence!"

Jolliet listened. He did not commit himself. The governor was not asking for opinions; he only wanted to air his own, to impress Louis with the importance of the English. He also knew that a good deal of what Bayly said was lamentably true: the English had been successfully outbidding the French for the best furs. If the French were to save the beaver trade, they would have to drive the English out of the Hudson Bay country, and do it quickly. It would be comparatively easy to do so, he thought. The forts were built more to keep out cold than gunfire, and faced the sea rather than the land. The English could not think that anyone would attack them from land, not from all those infinite miles of wasteland, tundra, spruce bogs, icy lakes, meandering rivers which went nowhere, land of the caribou, the white fox, and the raven. Nevertheless, Jolliet remembered how easily he and his party had slipped up to this very fort where he now sat as a guest, and had been undiscovered. They might have taken the fort in a trice if they had had the arms and men.

The long day passed. It was still broad daylight even when it must have been night. He had not known how late the sun was in the sky up here, how it set for only a short while in the night, and that light actually remained, lying silvery and mysterious across the tundra pools and making a glow on the gray rocks, lighting the bay and the river and the drifting icebergs. When dinner was served at ten, there was no real need to light the candles, though for sociability the governor lit a pair of the few he had left.

There was little enough for dinner, but it was nicely
served on English china, with elegant damask napkins and
cloth and the best silver, which an orderly had spent most
of the afternoon polishing. There was a brace of roast eider
ducks which had a decidedly fishy taste, being seabirds
whose only food was fish; some of the Madeira poured over
them while they roasted, however, helped somewhat to
modify the taste. There was also a piece of roasted caribou,
but it was tough and stringy. The cook had made yeast
bread and there were dried apples that had been stewed in
water and flavored with cinnamon. There was a sort of pud-
ding made of the baked-apple berries growing profusely on
the tundra, but poorly sweeted because sugar was scarce.
The governor apologized, but to Louis as well as to his men,
who had fared somewhat differently with the garrison on
salt pork, tough caribou, and hardtack, it was sufficient, and
they were thankful for it.

Although the governor next day urged Louis to stay
longer, he felt he must get back to Québec as soon as he
could to tell Duchesneau and Frontenac about what he had
learned. After finding out all he wanted to know, except
about the secret which, much to Louis's inner irritation, the
governor still would not divulge, they packed their gear in
the canoes. Jolliet needed a little food to carry them southward into a country where there would be more game. He
wanted to pay for what he took, but the governor refused
to accept any money. He gave them a bag of hardtack and
a sack of flour, the best he had and all he could spare. He
apologized again and again for such meager hospitality, and
hoped that they would return when his ship had come in.

He renewed his offer to Jolliet. If Louis would come as
his assistant, how wonderful life would be, really bearable
up here in the arctic wilds of this forsaken land! Together
they could accomplish so much. But Louis Jolliet refused

again, as politely as he could in the face of his rising impatience at the insistent governor. He was thankful when at last they had started off and away from the man's endless importunings, and paddled up the Rupert River. Governor Bayly, standing on the wind-punished shore, his coat flapping, his wig a tangle in the breeze off the bay, waved wistfully after them. The men of the fort stood watching impassively, saying nothing and not waving. But the governor saluted until the canoes had rounded the clay headland. They were alone again on the silence of the Rupert River.

Meanwhile in Québec, as summer waned, Claire-Françoise watched for the return of her husband. He had promised to be back before the baby was born and she had hoped that it would be so. She must have known by now that her husband was a restless soul, that the northern mysteries always called to him, that the sea and the river and the far horizon always held an allure which he could not escape. To keep him from being moody and unhappy, he must go when he wished, when adventure called to some forsaken waste of wilderness. God willing, he had always come back, and Claire trusted that he always would. Especially now, when she needed him.

It was a dangerous land, and the waters of the north were jealous waters, ready to claim the careless or those whom God did not protect. Claire knelt often before the family shrine, went daily to church, and prayed diligently.

The weeks passed, and the months. The child grew larger within her and the time of birth approached, and still her husband did not come. There was no word from him. Marie, her mother, took care of the other two, young Louis and Charles. Claire-Françoise was a strong young woman. She was well and the baby would come naturally, as most Canadian babies did, and that would be that, unless something unforeseen happened. But her love for the man who had gone away to the Arctic wilderness, and her growing worry, only added to her uneasiness as the tedious days passed.

Autumn colors were coming to the maples of Québec and the house on the Sous-le-Fort needed fires in all the fireplaces as the first frosts came. On a chill morning in September, Claire-Françoise felt her pains coming at short intervals. Her mother and the woman next door attended her; the baby came fast and Claire-Françoise was soon comfortable and slept soundly, the new infant cradled in her arm.

On October 5, 1679, the exploring party reached Québec. Young François by that time was three weeks old, healthy and hungry, when Louis Jolliet left his canoe down on the waterfront, and he and Zacharie and Guillaume Bissot hurried up the street to the house. Louis had almost forgotten that he would be a father again, and was half taken aback to find the newcomer already ensconced in the carved wood cradle which had rocked the children of the Jolliet and Bissot families.

He caught Claire-Françoise in his arms, and then the children, and his mother-in-law—of whom he was very fond and upon whom he relied to keep things going when he was away—and then the new baby. He would have to hump himself to make a living for them all. How wonderful if only the King would offer him what the governor of Hudson Bay had offered him!

Almost as in answer to the thought, the next year Louis Jolliet was given Anticosti Island in gratitude for his findings on Hudson Bay, as well as in belated recognition for mapping the Mississippi River.

Anticosti was formally presented "in consideration of his discovery of the Illinois country . . . and of the voyage which he has just made to Hudson Bay in behalf of and to the advantage of the Ferme du Roy of this colony."

Anticosti Island lay crosswise in the mouth of the Gulf of St. Lawrence, like a long, tapered ship—2,500,000 acres of rocks, cliffs, forests, stony beaches, rivers, waterfalls, and wild animals. He had put this island on that first map of his when he was a boy of thirteen, never even remotely thinking that he should someday be its proprietor!

Every ship coming in to the St. Lawrence had to pass Anticosti. It commanded the whole great harbor. It also commanded the best seal and cod fisheries; contained millions of feet of lumber, and the pelts of unknown numbers of animals ranging from moose to beaver.

Jolliet felt overwhelmed when he thought of this gift, and he made immediate plans to build a house, a fort, and a warehouse. It would be too wild and severe a place to live during the desperate winters which attacked this part of the world, but he and his family could spend the summers on Anticosti. They would be close to the fishing concessions of Mingan, Seven Islands, and Egg Island, only about twenty miles across the water to the north, and to the shores of the Gaspé forty-five miles southwest.

Only one fact may have caused him a little passing concern in contemplating this generous gift. If Anticosti commanded the Gulf and the harbor of Québec, then any enemy ships coming in to attack the French—always a possibility— would be certain to see and no doubt attack Anticosti first.

15

~~~~~

BOISSEAU

THERE WERE THOSE who objected to the good fortune of Louis Jolliet. "Favoritism" was the cry. One of the loudest objectors was Josias Boisseau, general manager in Canada of the Ferme du Domaine du Roy, controlling the trade in fishing and pelts. He was very definitely against all the favors paid to Jolliet and members of his family. To Jolliet lay rights to the concessions along all that north coast of the river, and now he had been given additional munificence in Anticosti— of all things, Anticosti, key to Canada!

Anticosti was a choice prize indeed. Governors and intendants of Canada knew it. They only gave rights to the island to those whom they wished especially to reward. Anticosti was a top prize, but Jolliet was the one who had done more, perhaps, than any other man for Canada and many agreed that he deserved it.

Boisseau, who was a notably noisy man, objected. He kept his voice down at first. On April 10, 1680, he went to the notary, Romain Bequet, and had him write out a document petitioning Duchesneau to annul the Anticosti concession made to Jolliet.

The document went to Duchesneau, the intendant, but it did little if any good. Boisseau, growing louder, went about town haranguing all who would listen to his complaints of the unfairness which was going on. What he was really alarmed about was the profitable trade which Jolliet and his associates were doing at Seven Islands and Mingan, which were very close to the boundaries of the King's Domain, and in which latter place their permits specifically did not apply.

Boisseau, however, was certain they were poaching. It would be so easy, he explained righteously, for these miscreants to slip into the King's Domain for seal, fish, and pelt, and carry their loot quickly in secret to their own territory, where it would look legal. He was very sure that something underhanded must be going on, though he couldn't prove it. He distrusted Louis Jolliet's assertions that all he did was legal and correct.

Then Boisseau, without mincing words, accused Jolliet of trading illegally with the Indians. This would make Jolliet no better than one of the *coureurs des bois* who for years had been doing an illicit and highly profitable black market in the finest beaver pelts. What with the English attracting the Indians to their own remote outposts and ships, and the bushrangers going out to the Indian villages, it was a wonder that any pelts at all came to the St. Lawrence. When Boisseau accused Louis Jolliet, whom he had known and been friendly with for years, of being a *coureur des bois,* he was insulting him, and he meant to.

The *coureurs des bois* had become a thorny issue between king and governor. One of Frontenac's first jobs when he came to Canada was to get rid of these undesirables. This he did, on the surface, at least. He did a great deal of talking about what was being done to remedy the situation, and then in 1674 he reported to Colbert that now only six terrified *coureurs des bois* were left. He claimed to have wiped out all the rest. It may have been, however, that Frontenac, whose underhanded dealings were a matter of some con-

jecture, was the one who most profited by the activities of
the bushrangers, and he had not really wiped them out at
all, only concealed their activities. At any rate, after report-
ing so virtuously to Colbert on what he had done, he let up
on his attacks on the *coureurs des bois,* and soon they
numbered more than eight hundred, all very active and
evidently well protected by Frontenac himself.

The King and Colbert discovered what was happening.
There were plenty of officials in Canada who were only too
eager to inform them of what the governor was doing. The
King then wrote him a reprimanding letter, insisting that
he must banish the offending ones at once and mend his own
ways. Frontenac hastily pinned the blame on the intendant,
but Duchesneau had proofs of his own innocence. He did
not hesitate to send them at once to the astute Colbert, who
really didn't like Frontenac anyway. Duchesneau was ab-
solved, and Frontenac severely scolded.

Josias Boisseau was in the service of Frontenac and admired him a great deal. He apparently would do anything
for his hero, and went about with his slanders against Jolliet and his associates in order to draw recrimination away
from Frontenac. In heaping blame and accusation on
Duchesneau and his friends, including Jolliet, Boisseau
busily dug up quantities of half truths and partial facts,
saying that it was not Frontenac's fault but the fault of
Duchesneau, La Chesnaye, the eminent Charles Le Moyne,
and Jacques Leber that the *coureurs des bois* were so active.
Boisseau stated that in 1679, under the false front of fishing,
La Chesnaye, who was Jolliet's uncle, had sent a ship commanded by Jolliet to "trade in forbidden places." And, went
on Boisseau, to make matters even more despicable, this
same Jolliet actually took the pelts he had got illicitly from
the Indians and traded them to the English! The English, of
all people, Boisseau cried. The treason of it!

The men called Lalande and Jolliet, brother-in-law and nephew of La Chesnaye, respectively, having taken ship toward Tadoussac, under the pretex of their Anticosti fishing concession, were accused and convicted after their return to Québec in the month of March of last year, 1680, of having enticed the Indians; and not only did they bring pelts to the English, but they even traded with the governor of Hudson Bay, and received gifts from him.

Duchesneau ignored the noise of Boisseau. He disdainfully put aside the petition as a piece of nonsense. He knew it was all a pack of fabrication designed to put Jolliet in a bad light and take from him the Mingan concession and the Anticosti gift. He could see what Boisseau was up to, and determined to keep the man at a safe distance. Duchesneau liked and admired Jolliet, knew that he was completely honest and devoted to the King's service. He knew, besides, that he could not have been at Hudson Bay when Boisseau charged, and that when Jolliet did go there it was certainly not to trade. He had not gone in a ship, but by canoe, and the purpose of the journey had been to find out the situation there. If Boisseau had heard that the English governor traded with them and gave them gifts, then he was only partly right. Governor Bayly had not traded with them because they brought nothing, and he had but little to give. The gifts he gave them were a pitiful sack of weevily flour and some bone-solid and mouse-gnawed hardtack to help them on their way home.

Duchesneau wished he could do something drastic about Boisseau and be rid of him permanently. He was a troublemaker who could be dangerous; he had made trouble before, but he was being noisiest now, and Duchesneau was irked by it. Maybe the time would come.

The curious thing about the whole matter was that in 1679 Boisseau and La Chesnaye had financed the trip Jolliet took to Hudson Bay. For some reason not explained and probably not to be known, the two had quarreled afterward, and by the time Jolliet came back, Boisseau was boiling with his injuries, real or fancied. He had always heretofore been friendly with the Jolliets, liked the young men of the family —Zacharie, in fact, had given him power of attorney before he went off to Hudson Bay.

Perhaps the real reason lay in the fact that Boisseau disliked Duchesneau because the latter was the political enemy of Frontenac; and Frontenac guided all Boisseau's actions. The whole thing may have been a sidewise blow at Duchesneau; and so Boisseau attacked Jolliet because he couldn't get at the man with more power. It was all a dismal mess. And there was so little Jolliet himself could do to defend himself against the stings and peckings of Boisseau.

The man would not be silenced. He wrote again to Duchesneau with more "evidence" against those guilty of the sin of "trading in forbidden territory," insisting that they should be fined two thousand livres, and their cargo and ship confiscated. They must be punished, Boisseau demanded, as an example to all other offenders, now and in the future. "Make an example of Louis Jolliet and Jacques Lalande! "

Duchesneau, knowing he had to do something to keep the peace and to quiet Boisseau, wrote an ordinance and signed it. In it he permitted Jolliet and Lalande to go off on another fishing expedition, but told them not to trade with the Indians or to entice them to trade, as Boisseau was sure they had been doing all the time, under penalty of two thousand livres and confiscation of ship and cargo.

This was a joke, but Duchesneau felt that it covered the situation, at least in the letter. But Boisseau was far from satisfied. Again he shouted. Duchesneau was exculpating the culprits, letting them go out again immediately with their ship to repeat their offenses and not even fining them a sou! It was a conspiracy against honest men. He declared he would hold a meeting of the Fermiers, his employers, to tell what was being done in Canada to ignore laws and justice and to permit obvious criminals to continue their nefarious crimes.

Duchesneau was getting out of patience, but he did his best to smooth down the ruffled Boisseau. He wrote another ordinance in which "these Lalande and Jolliet fellows" were required to pay a fine of five hundred livres and their ship to be confiscated. But they were never required to pay the fine, and their ship was confiscated only briefly enough to obey the letter of the law, and then they had it again. They set off down the St. Lawrence, free men, to carry on their legal business.

And when Jolliet and La Chesnaye, together with Jacques Lalande, on the ship named the *Ste Anne,* came back at last to Québec after an absence of all the summer of 1680, the ship again was well filled with beaver pelts, seal oil, dried codfish, and other items.

Boisseau howled again at the flagrant ignoring of the ordinances. He accused Jolliet and Lalande point-blank of having enticed the Indians to Seven Islands, of having traded in the forbidden limits of the King's Domain; he said that he now had evidence to prove that Jolliet had left men at Mingan in order to trade with the Indians all winter and thus further ruin the trade at Tadoussac.

Again Boisseau stormed to Duchesneau, and again the impatient and exasperated governor tried to quiet him down. This was becoming monotonous; it was irritatingly tiresome. He wished Boisseau would be recalled to France. In fact, perhaps he, Duchesneau, just might arrange such a thing. Yet to quiet Boisseau at the moment, he issued a private ordinance on September 27, 1680, permitting Lalande, Jol-

liet and their business partners to unload their pelts, and
then forbade them from then on to trade within the limits
of the King's Domain. Life went on as before.

Boisseau was not at all satisfied. He wrote to Colbert and
begged him to take up the matter with the King himself.
Somehow the King learned of the turmoil. He couldn't see
that it was as important as the man Boisseau claimed; nevertheless, he sent a letter to Duchesneau suggesting that perhaps he had shown a little too much favor to La Chesnaye,
and that, after all, it was Frontenac's place to determine
whether or not "the man called Jolliet" should be allowed
to leave Québec to trade and fish on the lower St. Lawrence.
That being that, the King dismissed the matter and went on
to complain vigorously and in no uncertain terms about the
coureurs des bois. He ended with the stern injunction that
it was absolutely required of Duchesneau to live on good
terms with the irascible Frontenac.

The King then wrote to Frontenac himself and repri-
manded him roundly and strongly for being too lenient with
the *coureurs des bois* and with other matters which he should
have long since attended to. The King accused him of sup-
porting men like that noisy Boisseau who was being such a
bother.

Frontenac was taken aback. He was no doubt suddenly
alarmed for his own personal safety and for his career. He
wrote unhappily back to Colbert that he had only been trying to do his duty as he saw it.

While all these messages passed slowly back and forth
across the leisurely Atlantic, Josias Boisseau was still in Québec. When he was told to let up on the Jolliet affair and
forget it, his temper was not improved. He had always been
noted for his rages. There was a day in the court of law
when a *coureur des bois* would not alter his testimony, sitting stubbornly with his arms folded and an insolent, stony

expression on his dark, hairy face. Boisseau had gone into one of his rages. He threatened to throw the man out of the window, though the *coureur des bois* was a large man who could with ease have tossed Boisseau from the same window. Boisseau danced around in fury as the man sat in silence, and then threatened to lock him up in the cellar and let him starve to death.

Still the man said nothing. When the court was dismissed, Boisseau came up behind the man as he was slouching down the steps and kicked him, so that the bushranger, caught off guard and off balance, sprawled down the steps. Boisseau, passing him in impotent fury, leaned down and slapped the man, and, as the report in Québec said in shocked tones: *"jurant horriblement contre Dieu et comme un lyon."*

In November, 1681, the terrible-tempered M. Boisseau was called back to France. Louis Jolliet retained all rights to Mingan, Seven Islands, and Anticosti.

16

~~~~~~

FRONTENAC

Ten years in the life of a man can mean years of success or failure, of heartbreak or joy. Ten years in the life of a country may also hold great triumph, or may bring that land to the nadir of its power and hope. Thus, in the decade between 1680 and 1690, as Louis Jolliet spent most of his time at his work and in rearing his family, Canada, during those same years, saw many things happen to it, and very few of them were good. To many people, it seemed that the triumphs of Canada's earlier years when Jean Talon reorganized the government had been lost in blind defeat and impending doom.

To Louis and Claire Jolliet, four more children were born, completing the family—Marie-Geneviève in 1681, Anne in 1682, Jean-Baptiste in 1683, Claire in 1685. There are extended records of the lives of six of the children and of their descendants, but of Anne nothing is known more than that she was born and baptized. Perhaps Anne Jolliet died at an early age, even shortly after birth. The six remaining children were evidently strong and handsome and lively. In 1683, an orphaned youth named Michel De Sorcis, Jr., was hired as a manservant in the household and in a little while had become almost as one of the family.

In the year when little Anne stayed so briefly on the scene,

the ambitious and often unreliable La Salle finally reached
the mouth of the Mississippi and claimed the whole vast
valley for the King of France. That same year King Louis
XIV, having had his fill of Frontenac's troublemaking and
the constant bickering and outright trouble between him
and the intendant, Duchesneau, recalled Frontenac to
France. The King had had all he could take.

The old warrior must have been shocked by this sudden
recall and obvious reprimand. His wife, too, who had remained all those years in France, must not have been particularly pleased. Life was more interesting and far more
peaceful for Anne Frontenac when the count was safely on
the western side of the Atlantic, where he could roar and
complain and make love and cause trouble without annoy-
ing her and her own fascinatingly complicated life at court.

Louis Buade, Count de Frontenac, nevertheless had come
back to France. Mournfully, he could not see how Canada
would exist without him. Most of Canada, however, seemed
to be very happy to be rid of him.

But Canada did not, in fact, get along very well. When his
imposing militant figure departed on the ship bound for
France, the people knew that though he may have been
hated by many, had been perhaps dishonest in his dealings,
it was this powerful man who had been holding Canada together. It was he of whom the Indians stood in awe. And
now with this strength gone from New France, and Duchesneau gone too, the Iroquois Confederacy could feel a relaxing of their long discipline to the word of the great Onontio.
The Indian situation almost immediately grew ugly.

Meanwhile, Frontenac and Duchesneau were followed by
a succession of incompetent men who served but indiffer-
ently as governors and intendants in a complex situation
calling for courage, knowledge, tact, and the long view, but
who were not blessed with these abilities. La Barre, a lawyer

and a braggart, who had accepted the new post with the idea of making money out of it, and the new intendant, De Meules, who was no better, arrived in Québec. With their coming, the colony began to shrivel and to fall on hard and bitter times.

La Barre's relations with the Indians were poor indeed. He had none of Frontenac's confidence and power to awe the Iroquois. They looked with scorn on the new governor, quickly taking his measure, and they viciously set about returning to their old regime of killing and burning along the St. Lawrence. The frightened La Barre called for troops; but when they came, he led them so poorly that the Indian situation grew rapidly worse instead of better. The King, at last, posted on events by the tattling De Meules, hastily recalled the ineffectual Governor La Barre and sent over Denonville to take his place.

Denonville, however, rapidly made a shambles out of what La Barre had left him. He waged war on the Senecas and Iroquois and attacked the English settlements. He sent an expedition to make war on the English forts on Hudson Bay —forts considerably strengthened since Louis Jolliet visited the one on the Rupert River. The French forces were badly whipped by the English.

At about this time, also, Denonville, following the unwise suggestion of Louis XIV, sent Iroquois captives to be galley slaves, a fate equal to any Iroquois torture itself, where many of them died. The wrath of the Iroquois at home flamed even greater than before. They staged a hideous raid on the town of Lachine above Montréal, and spent a long night of terror in burning and torturing its people. Inhabitants of nearby Montréal, seeing the fires and hearing the Indian yells and the screams of the captives before they mercifully died, shuddered in the fear that they surely would be next.

Further horrors were being planned against the people

along the St. Lawrence by Indians farther west, when La Durantaye out at Michilimackinac heard rumors of what was intended. It was December, 1689. He needed to send word at once to warn the cities along the St. Lawrence. He needed a man who knew the waterways intimately and could get through in spite of all difficulties along the way. It was winter and travel would be hard.

Zacharie Jolliet volunteered to carry the word to Montréal. For some reason which history does not explain, Zacharie was at Michilimackinac in Lake Michigan at the time. He may have been trading, or he may have been in La Durantaye's service. In either case, it was Zacharie who, with one man accompanying him in a canoe, set off to carry the news of the Indian uprising.

Not many men would have dared to traverse the northern wilderness at this time of year, but evidently a Jolliet could. Zacharie and his companion were combating not only freezing rivers, deep cold, and Indians, however; they were racing against the pressure of time. They must get to Montréal before the western Iroquois. If the rivers froze too soon, the two would be compelled to go on foot, which was more dangerous and time-consuming.

They must have taken the short route—Lake Huron, French River, Lake Nipissing, Ottawa River. They fought the rapids, the slower waters which already had iced; they avoided brushes with Indians, rested as little as possible, went on night and day. Pushed to the utmost limit in strength, they reached Montréal in less than a month. The colony was warned. A force of soldiers sent out from the city met the Indians and prevented an attack.

Montréal was capable of defense now—miraculously, Frontenac had been sent back to remedy the dreadful state of affairs in Canada. Whether or not Zacharie Jolliet liked Frontenac, it must have been a relief to him, whatever his political leanings, to know that the competent governor was there to direct maneuvers and to hold off the Indians. No one could be sure of those weaker ones, De Meules, La Barre, or Denonville. Of Frontenac, yes.

For the King had decided, after seven years of seeing Canada fall apart under incompetent leadership, that he had been wrong to remove Frontenac. Obviously his successors had done nothing constructive, and under Denonville matters had, indeed, reached a most fearful pass. So Frontenac, late in 1689, was ordered to return. And if some people had been glad to see him leave in 1682, they were even happier to see him back. They had been fearing for their very existence, now that the Indians were closing in, while the massacre at Lachine was still fresh. No one knew what would be done next by the rash and incautious Denonville who had only worsened the situation for Canada with every move he made.

He had even agreed, in desperation as everything he touched seemed to go wrong, to permit the Iroquois Confederation to take back French land along the lakes. To placate the Iroquois, he had promised to blow up Fort Frontenac at Cataraqui and throw the cannons into the water. The Indians were licking their lips at how they had intimidated this weak Onontio. They knew they could never have done so with the old one, Frontenac.

But now Frontenac had come back. The first thing he learned when he came ashore was that Denonville had ordered Fort Frontenac destroyed—his fort at Cataraqui which he, Frontenac, had built with incredible speed and of incredible size mightily to impress the watching Iroquois!

The governor raged. His fiery disposition had not cooled during his absence. For his beloved fort to be wrecked so wantonly by Frenchmen themselves, leaving the hardly won land for the Iroquois to take over—it was insupportable! He sent out men at once to stop the action, but they were too late. The magnificent fort had been blown up and the cannons already lay in the water. Frontenac called down imprecations on the absent Denonville.

The governor, however, wasted no time in letting the Iroquois know that he had indeed returned. Matters along the St. Lawrence were well in hand when Zacharie Jolliet arrived with news of further Indian trouble. But Montréal, thus warned in time, was defended.

During the years when Frontenac was away, Louis Jolliet had been busy. He had quietly carried on his business in the fisheries. Codfish was one of the great commercial products of New France, and to deal in cod meant profits.

Codfish was much sought as food, both at home and as an export. French fishermen had come long before Champlain set a colony along the St. Lawrence, and had fished off the Grand Banks and the islands of St. Pierre and Miquelon near Newfoundland. The cod was a firm-fleshed creature which when dried and salted would keep almost indefinitely. In a time of no refrigeration, protein food of this sort was invaluable as supplies to be taken on all distant endeavors, exploration, settling remote colonies, stocking ships' stores for long voyages. Catholic Europe, besides, in observing numerous religious fast days, ate great quantities of fish each year. Most kinds had to be eaten almost at once. The cod lasted almost forever.

Codfish caught near Canada were large and excellent; they were some of the best in the world. Fishermen knew where to find the greatest numbers by watching for shoals of small capelin, the favorite food of the cod, and thus usually used for bait. Where the capelin swarmed, the larger fish were not far behind.

Jolliet's ship went out during the season to bring back tons of cod. Some were salted aboard ship, other catches brought fresh to Anticosti where the fish were split, gutted, and laid on racks to dry.

Louis had built himself an extensive establishment on Anticosti. There was not only the house, large enough for the whole family and half a dozen servants, but a fort, and several sheds and warehouses where pelts, casks of seal oil, and the dried or salted fish could be kept until autumn when the family bark went back to Québec for the winter. Anticosti was a delightful place for the entire family to spend the summer. Not only was the air pleasantly sea-cooled during the warm months, but there were virtually no mosquitoes or black flies on the entire island, a great contrast to the hordes of insects besieging fishermen and trappers ashore. At times Jolliet let the older boys go exploring inland, where they found the swift, clear, cold rapids of the Jupiter River passing below its white sandstone cliffs. They discovered Vaureal Falls leaping over its precipice to a canyon deep in the rock, and found many beaver dams farther down the rivers. There was a regular supply of pelts to be had right here on their own island, the Jolliet boys would exult, except that they could never come in winter when the pelts were prime, and their father had told them not to bring in any more of the meager summer furs.

There was plenty of work for everyone on the island. The codfish on the racks must be turned, must be covered or hastily brought in if storms came or thick fogs prevented drying. At a distance from the house, the servants and some of the Indians who worked for Louis kept a fire going under the try pots, rendering out seal oil. Claire-Françoise hated the thick black smoke, especially when the wind changed and brought it into the house. Marie, her mother, had a good deal to say, too, when the seal-oil smoke blew across her clean laundry flapping in the sea wind.

But Anticosti was a sweet, idyllic place, as wild and free

and remote from the rest of the world as if it were a desert island in some far sea. It was true that Louis and the men were often gone for weeks at a time, but the women and children felt safe on the island. It was miles distant from any hostile Indians of the mainland, far indeed from any enemy.

It was when Louis was out on one of his long fishing voyages that he ventured farther north than he had ever been before. He had sailed along the north shore of the Gulf of St. Lawrence, up through the straits of Belle Isle between Newfoundland and the mainland, and had found himself along the coast of Labrador.

Here were grim, unmapped shores whose dark cliffs and headlands seemed devoid of any life but that of the birds and animals. The cliffs were, indeed, alive with nesting colonies of sea birds. But it was the fact that here were uncharted shores, coastlines without any map to guide navigators, which awoke in Louis once again his deep longing for adventure, for maps to make. He had worked sporadically on revising his Mississippi River map and various charts of the St. Lawrence, but had tried to keep his attention on his work, his family, the music he played during the winter for services at the Cathedral of Québec. The wild shores of Labrador stirred the old restlessness, as if it had never been absent at all.

17

~~~~~~~~

DISASTER

Less than a year after Zacharie Jolliet came to warn Montréal about the impending Indian attack, English ships came north to the Bay of Fundy and attacked Port Royal in Acadia. Without any anticipation of invasion and without adequate protection, Governor Meneval had given up so easily to the invaders that the English commander, Phips, felt that all the French were cowards. The rest of New France, he decided, would be a simple feat to conquer.

Therefore, since the trial raid on Acadia in April, 1690, had presented so little trouble, Sir William Phips, a large man, born of a poor family in Massachusetts and but lately knighted, was puffed with his victory. It would be easy, he assured his peers, to continue up the coast, sail into the St. Lawrence, and take Québec and Montréal as simply as he had taken Port Royal.

A shipload of ammunition, ordered from England for the impending attack on Québec, did not come. Phips was impatient at delay and refused to wait. It was already August, 1690, and he knew that winter came early to the country along the St. Lawrence. If he was to have time to sail up there and back home before severe storms set in and the river froze, he would have to do it without waiting for the extra ammunition. Anyway, he naïvely doubted that he would have need of it—Acadia had been taken so easily.

If all the French were as easy as the Acadians and that vapid Meneval, the powder, shot, and cannon balls would only take up space. Nevertheless, to be on the safe side, he called for all the war supplies in Boston and its environs. He sailed from Nantasket on August 9 with thirty-two ships of varying tonnage, and about two thousand men. His flagship, the *Six Friends*, carried forty-four guns, while the *John and Thomas*, the *Swan*, and the *American Merchant* were well armed, too.

There was no secret about what was going on or what Sir William Phips was intending to do. He and his men had already planned in detail how to divide the spoils of Québec, and had even arranged for eventual disposition of the rich silver candlesticks which were said to be in the Cathedral de Notre Dame. Boston looked forward to the return of the hero who would have put the French in their place, punished their audacity in raiding English settlements, and confiscated their popish paraphernalia.

But too many people knew about the expedition. The Indians knew, and the information traveled north. Rather belatedly, however, on October 10, two months after the fleet had departed for Canada, a message was brought to the Count de Frontenac who was visiting at that time in Montréal. He was to come at once to Québec. *Les Bostonnais* were on their way to attack the city.

The ships had sailed steadily up the coast, rounded Nova Scotia and the New Brunswick shores, and were heading into the Gulf of St. Lawrence on an October day, when they discovered the great, grim whaleback of Anticosti's island wilderness athwart the way.

The Jolliets on Anticosti had heard about the English raid on Acadia in the spring. It was over, and there was no suggestion that the invaders would come back for any further spoils. The summer had been peaceful on the island, and soon, as autumn emblazoned the aspens on the island with pure yellow and the birches with gold and the sugar-plum trees with purple and maroon, it would be time to go back to Québec for the winter.

On a bright, sparkling October day when the sea was exceptionally blue and the sky even bluer without a particle of fog in sight, while the gulls and gannets were coasting past with wild cries, and rotund seals gathered to sun themselves with their young on the rocks along the south shore of the island, Marie Lalande and Claire-Françoise Jolliet looked up suddenly from their work to see sails on the horizon. On a south wind, strange ships were bearing quickly toward the island.

The two startled women knew that three supply ships were due from France in October; but these were not French vessels, and there were far more than three. It seemed to the horrified eyes of Marie and her daughter that the whole south horizon was full of advancing sails. They could only belong to the English.

Marie called to her grandchildren, Jean-Baptiste, Marie-Geneviève, and Claire, who had been helping turn the codfish on the racks. Their mother rounded up the four menservants and a maid and ran with petticoats flying in the wind down to the wharf where the Jolliet bark lay at anchor. She screamed to the men to get up sail, quickly, quickly, that ships were coming up from the south—surely the English—and they were heading straight for the island.

The men ran up the sails. Claire-Françoise was thankful that a bark required so few men to handle it. She wished desperately that Louis and the three oldest, Louis, Charles, and François, were at home to help her in this terrible emergency, but they were all away in La Chesnaye's bark,

fishing, and were not due home for a week or two. Louis
liked to stay out until the breath of winter seemed to be
sensed by the cod, and they moved slowly southward. There
is, in fact, no record of just where Louis Jolliet was at that
tense moment in his family's life—fishing, or up along Labrador—where? But he was not on Anticosti.

Marie Lalande dashed back into the house only long
enough to snatch up the holy figures and crucifix from the
family shrine, the fresh bread just out of the big brick out-
door oven, and some meat, all of which she tumbled into a
tablecloth and then piled in cloaks and other garments for
her daughter, herself, and the children. She closed the door,
put the bar in place, and went out the secret back door. She
wished there were time to load pelts and other goods from
the warehouse—Louis had thousands of livres tied up in
those supplies—but the ships were coming alarmingly closer,
and she dared not take the time. She ran after the children
down the stony path and across the rocks to the wharf, and
onto the bark where Claire and Michel De Sorcis had the
men ready to cast off. The sails were up, the wind opened
them, the anchor was raised, and the bark sped off to the
north. Claire didn't know where they should go; but twenty
miles across the water lay their house at Mingan. If they
could only reach it in time, they might be safe.

Sir William Phips on the *Six Friends* was in no hurry
to reach Québec. He could take time out along the way to
secure a little extra booty. When he saw the long, wooded
island of Anticosti dead ahead, he decided that there might
be habitations ashore which could be plundered. Then he
saw sails of a bark fleeing to the north. Let it go. They could
catch it later. The *Six Friends* rounded the point of the island
and turned into the bay where the Jolliet wharves stood
deserted. Up the hill he saw the big house, the fort, the

warehouses. They all looked exceptionally wealthy, and quite deserted. There were no people in sight, but no doubt something of value had been left in the buildings.

His men scrambled ashore on the smooth stones and up the slope to the log structures which Louis Jolliet had built with so much labor and care. The men broke open the warehouse and exclaimed at all the riches inside—piles of neatly stretched and stacked pelts of beaver, moose, otter, and fox; casks of seal oil; boxes and bags containing knives, beads, and other trade items for the Indians. The men loaded everything into the hold of the *Six Friends,* regretting the space the ammunition supplies required. They cleaned out everything of value from the warehouses; the drying codfish on the racks in the late south sun, however, they disdained. Holding their noses against the offensive smell, they kicked thousands of pounds of drying fish in a tumbling white avalanche down the slope to the beach.

The raiders went into the fort, but found little there except some powder and balls and a half a dozen muskets. They took everything they found, however, even a box of candles. Others broke open the door of the house, smashed Claire's dishes, dragged out clothing and bedding. Marie Lalande had taken the best things, though they really had kept little that was valuable out at the summer place on Anticosti. The good silver, linens, and china were in Québec.

At the rail of the fleeing bark, Marie, Claire-Françoise, Michel De Sorcis, the children, and the men watched as long as they could see the island. They could see figures of men running about, saw them busily carrying things down to the ship, and shuddered at all that Louis and the business would lose.

Then they saw a pillar of black smoke and sudden leaping flames against the calm blue of the October sea and sky, and Marie exclaimed: "Mon Dieu, the house!"

The men ashore were running about like so many Iroquois, setting fire to house and sheds and warehouses and fort. The smoke rose swirling to the sky. The girls wept. Claire-Fran-çoise held them close. Marie Lalande cursed the English and begged divine retribution upon the beastly raiders.

Though the bark had had a head start, it was overtaken before dark by the *Six Friends*. In despair Claire-Françoise, Marie, and the anxious men aboard knew they were caught. Grappling irons were thrown over to secure the smaller ship to the larger. Sir William Phips, with considerable politeness when he saw that ladies were aboard, and with white gloves conspicuous on his large hands, ceremoniously assisted the furious Mme Lalande and the wet-eyed Mme Jolliet, and the maidservant, and the frightened children, aboard the *Six Friends*. The men followed in silence.

Sir William ordered some of his men to take over the Jolliet bark which he thereupon commandeered and sailed, later on, back to Boston. Mme Lalande, an outspoken and explosive person on occasion, as soon as her feet were safely on the deck of the *Six Friends,* proceeded to give Sir William a dressing-down in fluent and furious French which, no doubt, was largely lost upon the man who knew not a word of this ill-thought-of language. He could not, however, have failed to have sensed the drift of the diatribe, and when Marie Lalande finally ran out of words, Claire-Françoise took over the tirade and embellished it with a good many sentiments of her own.

The Frenchwomen, even though enemies of the invaders, were looked at with considerable admiration by the Boston men. Even the older of the two women was most attractive and full of life, and the sailors chuckled and nudged each other as Marie lashed out at the big red-faced Sir William, who was a young man and not accustomed to such Gallic

fury in the more circumspect women of Boston, certainly
not from his meek and wealthy wife.

Rant and berate as they would, Marie and Claire, as well
as the crew of the bark, were prisoners.

Instead of continuing promptly up the narrowing channel
of the St. Lawrence to attack Québec at once, Sir William
ordered his ships to anchor in the dark waters at Tadoussac,
at the mouth of the Saguenay. Here he and his officers spent
a number of days in working out a plan of surrender for
Québec, again apportioning the various shares of the spoils.

By this time, it was well known in Québec that *les Bostonnais* were only two or three days' sail from Québec itself.
Frontenac, meanwhile, had been far from idle. The old giant
had been spurred into a fury of preparing for a siege. Before he left Montréal, he had sent word to the governor of
that city, M. Bonnevue de Callières, to come with every
available armed man he could muster, and to come in a
hurry. Frontenac proceeded rapidly by canoe down the river
and got to Québec on the fourteenth, to find that Prévost
had the defenses well begun, had built barricades of earth,
stone, and tree trunks around the rear of the city and along
the St. Charles River.

The people of the lower town were being evacuated. The
nuns on the hill were digging holes in the convent garden
in which to bury the church silver and other valuables. The
superior was trying desperately to make room for all the
women and children who were already seeking shelter in
the convent during the impending attack. Batteries of guns,
ranged around the ramparts, pointed black mouths down at
the harbor, waiting for the ships to appear.

The coming of Frontenac calmed the rising panic. The
older people still remembered how it was when the English
had attacked Québec when Champlain was governor, and
how terrible was the starving time, and how many had died

of hunger rather than bullets. But now with the furious Frontenac competently striding the stones of Québec, things fell into place. People were tense, but the panic was gone.

Frontenac dispatched M. de Grandville in a hurry down the river in a launch to keep watch on the approaching vessels and to send word back when he saw them. But Sir William discovered the somewhat inept M. de Grandville on his spying mission, and promptly added him to his group of prisoners. Mme Lalande no doubt sneered at him for being such a careless ninny as to have been captured. And what good would he do Frontenac and Québec now?

When no word came from de Grandville, there was nothing for the people of Québec to do but watch and wait. Then on the sixteenth of October, when at dawn there were the dim shapes of sails hanging limply in the fog, and indistinct hulls riding in the misty river, Frontenac and the people, watching from the ramparts of the upper town, knew that the time had come.

No guns were fired. The French waited. When the wind got up enough to bring the *Six Friends* and other ships close to the lower town, a small boat was put out. A young ensign climbed smartly down the ladder and, under a flag of truce, was rowed to shore. He bore with him papers stating Phips's elaborate terms of surrender. It had been assumed that Frontenac and Québec would surrender as easily as poor frightened Governor Meneval and Port Royal.

Frontenac, who bore not the slightest resemblance to Meneval, sent men down to the harbor to greet the envoy. They promptly blindfolded him and sent the small boat away from shore. No Englishman but the envoy would be allowed to set foot in Québec.

The bewildered young ensign, having been told that he had been blindfolded so that he could not see the extent of

French defenses, was led by the gleeful French over rocks and logs and barricades, the longest way around, while a few soldiers did a lot of noisy marching and clanking of muskets within earshot, as if there were a whole regiment drilling. There was considerable ostentatious shouting and ordering about as they brought the Boston man up the steeps of Mountain Hill. He stumbled and slipped and grew more and more furious behind his blindfold.

They led him up the long stairs to the great hall of Chateau St. Louis, where Frontenac, the Le Moynes, and other dignitaries waited, all in their finest uniforms and plumed hats and swords. It was an imposing scene which met the blinking eyes of the angry young emissary from the ship. He had dust on his knees and fury in his heart. But it was a very different sort of gathering from that which Sir William had blandly anticipated, or which he had led the young man to expect. He had told him that the French were cowards who would give up at the first show of power, and for him therefore to be forceful and to show at once who was master.

But it was not easy for the young man to put on a dominant air under the overwhelming glower of the indignant Count de Frontenac. With him, stern and implacable in the face of the threat to the rock of Québec, to which they had brought civilization, were Jacques and Charles Le Moyne, and Claude de Ramezay, and the Sieur de Subercase, and M. Valrenne, the bishop, and the intendant, and many more. The rest would be coming in soon as reinforcements. Callières was on his way from Montréal at that moment with eight hundred men, and with him were coming the strong men of New France—the Sieur du Lhut, and Durantaye from Michilimackinac, and Nicholas Perrot from Green Bay, while coming back from an expedition to Hudson Bay were the Sieur d'Iberville and the Sieur Maricourt, sons of Charles Le Moyne.

The young envoy had courage. He faced the determined, hard-eyed, elegantly dressed throng, watching him in silence as he unrolled the paper on which was written the outrageous terms of surrender—surrender, Sir William had stated, within an hour, or be destroyed.

Frontenac was seething, but he held his temper as the interpreter read the preposterous document. He certainly would not sign this incredible paper, nor write any of his own terms to the upstart Phips. He considered Sir William a stupid fool, and told the young ensign so. As the young man's eyes were being blindfolded again, preparatory to returning him to the waterfront with Frontenac's reply, the governor said haughtily, in dismissal: "A man like me is not to be summoned after this fashion. Let him do his best; I will do mine! My answer lies in the mouths of my cannon!"

The young man was taken back to the waiting boat—again the long way around, while people jostled him as if the place were as crowded as on market day. Later, aboard the *Six Friends*, he gave a glowing account of the glories and size of the Québec which he had not seen at all, but had only heard and felt.

Sir William waited all day—much longer than the specified hour he had given on the surrender paper—for Frontenac to capitulate, and finally decided that the fellow really had meant it, and that he was not going to give up. Phips thereupon sent Major Walley ashore at Beauport, below Québec, with a troop of men who were to come in on the rear and surprise the city, to prepare the way for the sea attack.

But the landing was through slimy mud and cold water; there was a bitter chill in the air and a snapping-cold sunset as the men waded to their midriffs to get to shore. Then the 1,300 English were suddenly fired upon by French forces under Maricourt and Ste. Hélène. The English, however, continued on to shore and finally by night they had entrenched themselves within reach of the St. Charles River and, hopefully, still within touch of the fleet.

Phips had intended to wait until Walley secured the rear of Québec before he would begin the bombardment from the front. But Phips was always one to hurry things at the wrong time, to delay when speed was vital. Now he went ahead before hearing of Walley's success, if any.

Phips's guns opened fire on the city on the rock. The *Six Friends*, still holding prisoner the alarmed but staunch Marie Lalande and Claire-Françoise and the three young Jolliet children, moved in closer to the city. From a porthole, Marie and Claire could see the very street where they themselves lived, the fine stone house up on Rue Sous-le-Fort. When Phips's guns opened fire, the women covered their ears at the horrid thundering.

In the upper town, the cannon balls from the English bombardment dropped harmlessly into yards and streets. Some fell into the garden and courtyard of the convent, where the resourceful Reverend Mother Juchereau, the superior, ordered the terrified nuns to gather up the spent balls in their aprons. There were twenty-six balls in all, according to the Reverend Mother's unimpassioned account, and these were trundled back in a hand cart by one of the bravest of the nuns, to the Québec cannoneers on the ramparts. They forthwith fired back the Boston balls with Québec's compliments to the ships.

A ball splintered one of the masts on the *Six Friends*. Marie and Claire, below decks, heard the crash just above their heads, and they fell to their knees with frantic prayers for preservation from certain death in the river. To be slain, besides, by Canadian cannon balls in front of Québec itself would be an insupportable grief and something of a disgrace besides.

Phips in some alarm moved the ships away to a greater

distance to get out of range of Frontenac's guns which were raking masts and decks. The French had the additional advantage of being able to fire down onto the harbor, while the ships' guns had to fire upward at a slant, with indifferent success. This very fact was one of the points which caused Champlain, years before, to select this promontory for his city.

Moving away from the French gunners' range also put Phips and his vessels well out of their own firing range on the city. He had no idea how Major Walley and his land forces were faring. It was certain that there was no undue turmoil in the upper town to indicate that any counteraction was coming in from the rear. Phips also began to realize with some alarm that his supply of powder was rapidly diminishing.

That night the temperature dropped. The St. Charles River froze hard enough for Walley's men, cold and hungry and disgusted with conquests in Canada, to cross over. Many were ill. Smallpox, brought up from Boston, had broken out among them. When finally the majority got back to the St. Lawrence and regained their ships, without having engaged in any appreciable combat, all notion of fighting the French had faded. Besides, when Walley reported that winter was rapidly coming on this benighted northern land, and that food was scarce ashore, Sir William Phips finally realized that he himself hadn't enough supplies to feed and clothe his two thousand men, even if they did manage to take Québec.

There grew in Sir William—and had been very evident in most of his men for some time—the urgent need to get out of this place, to escape before he was trapped by ice or wrecked by storm. The whole thing had been a failure. Already a rising wind had torn loose some of the anchors. Splintered masts must be repaired. With one accord, the

Boston fleet fled down the river toward the Île d'Orléans to get out of the wind and away from the guns.

Frontenac watched them go. He hoped *les Bostonnais* were really going home, but he could not be sure. He sent the valiant M. Subercase to follow and watch, to see what happened next.

When the fleet loaded with the defeated English moved away from Québec and seemed likely to be going briskly home to Boston, Marie Lalande and Claire Jolliet got up off their knees in alarm. They had endured the trial of watching their beloved city bombarded, had with amazement seen the growing discouragement of the Boston men, had been prayerfully thankful when they suddenly realized that they were still alive, even though captives in that fleet.

While the battered ships lay anchored in the lee of the Île d'Orléans, Mme Lalande, through an interpreter, presented her plea to Phips who, though weary, chagrined, and very much anguished at the failure of the siege, nevertheless listened as the forceful Frenchwoman talked. He probably had little choice in the matter when Mme Lalande decided to speak.

Here they were, she said, gesturing, prisoners on the English ship, while in Québec were certain English prisoners taken in the French raids on Schenectady and Salmon Falls and Casco. These people did not want to remain in Canada any more than she and her daughter wished to remain with *les Bostonnais*. Why not, then, she said eloquently, carry out an exchange of prisoners while they were all still here, so handy for the exchange? Thus Sir William would be feeding his own people on the journey home, instead of the enemy!

Sir William was too tired to argue. He sent a messenger to Frontenac with the terms: an equal exchange of prisoners. It did not seem to occur to Phips, at least not at that time, that he was exchanging mostly able-bodied men, plus two women, three children, and the estimable M. de Grandville, for a group of women and children captured by the French; that the Canadians were benefiting more than he, in man power. But he was only glad to have it over with; thankful, too, no doubt, to be rid of the voluble Mme Lalande and her equally voluble daughter.

The English colonists were rowed out to the *Six Friends*, and Marie, Claire, the children, M. de Grandville, the sailors and servants from Anticosti, climbed down and were taken ashore. The Jolliets found their way to the house on the Rue Sous-le-Fort, let themselves in—the place was undamaged—and collapsed in the blessed safety of home. Their one thought now was of the safety of Louis and the boys and Jacques Lalande—if only they did not meet the retreating English.

As the ships went away, Frontenac allowed himself to relax and smile again. He and his men drank a toast to victory and wished never to see the dastardly *Bostonnais* again, a feeling which was no doubt a mutual one. In Québec's lower town the church which had been built in 1688 was renamed Notre Dame des Victoires. Masses of thanksgiving were held in this and in all the churches along the St. Lawrence.

But although the English had fled, Frontenac was still beset with worry. There were the three French supply ships which were due to arrive any day. There was the ugly possibility that the English fleet would meet the incoming vessels somewhere out in the gulf and would take all three captive. If this happened, then Phips would have ruined Québec more thoroughly than any mere bombardment, as the Kirkes had done, for food, clothing, medical supplies, and many other necessities were coming in from France on these last ships of the season.

Frontenac hastily dispatched canoes to slip ahead of the warships and intercept the French vessels. And there they were, looming in the fog near the great purple-gray cliffs of the Saguenay. Hastily moving into the protection of this river and its headlands, the French ships were hidden in the fog, so well concealed that even though Phips was aware that ships were close by, he could not discover their whereabouts, and went on his way.

All along his route down the St. Lawrence to the sea, the autumn fogs and storms upon him, Phips and the fleet met trouble. One vessel, the *Mary*, ran aground on a reef alongside Anticosti and was tossed by the storm onto the rocky beach. Most of the men survived, but were marooned without food or shelter. They were at the mercy of the sea blasts of the coming winter.

The ship was ruined, so they built a hut from some of its salvaged planks. They had to ration what little food they could find, but of sixty men, forty perished on the island which they had plundered of Jolliet's food. They had, besides, in burning his houses, destroyed the shelter which could have saved them.

The few survivors built a skiff and fixed a sail salvaged from the wreck, and in March the handful set off to find home. Somehow, someway, most of them got there after two long, dreadful, and incredible months at sea.

In the spring of 1691, Louis Jolliet came back to Anticosti to assess the damages to his property. He had no hope of finding anything left. Marie and Claire had given him a full account of the disaster, yet even so he was shocked at the total ruin he found. Sailing along the shores, he came upon the wreck of the *Mary*, and the poor hut made of its timbers, and the sparsely covered graves . . . and wondered at the uselessness of so much waste of materials and men.

As for Louis Jolliet, much of the hard-won success and prosperity of his years of work had been wiped out. All he possessed now remained in the house in Québec, and in the scanty buildings at Mingan and Seven Islands, the latter mere camping and trading places.

His ship was gone, taken by *les Bostonnais;* his buildings, his supplies, the pelts by which he would have profited, the thousands of pounds of codfish which Phips's men had so wantonly scattered down the cliff to the gulls—all were gone. But he was alive, and Claire-Françoise was alive, and the children. Life and hope and courage—in Canada that was all anyone needed. He was forty-five, still young enough to pick up the thread of business and rebuild his fortunes.

Looking at the charred, snow-beaten, rain-lashed ruins of his property at the rim of the Anticosti wilderness, Louis Jolliet felt an emptiness, but he would not admit defeat.

18

~~~~~

LABRADOR

HE HAD NO SOONER begun to rebuild on Anticosti than disaster struck again. Marauding English ships in 1691 came suddenly into the Gulf of St. Lawrence and, not attempting any attack on Québec, simply raided the holdings of Jolliet and Lalande at Mingan and on Seven Islands. As the Boston fleet had done on Anticosti only the year before, the English plundered everything of value, the warehouses were emptied and burned, the houses looted and destroyed. Everything was gone. Jolliet had put up a new warehouse on Anticosti, had borrowed from his stand-by, La Chesnaye, to buy trade goods, had secured the use of another bark, had felt that he might get back on his feet again.

The second attack left him all but discouraged, but still not so hopeless that he sat back in defeat. While there were still codfish in the sea, and shores to explore, and maps to make, he refused to be ruined: not with the mystery of the north unsolved, and he still alive to solve it.

On Louis Jolliet's brief excursion up along the coast of southern Labrador, he had been fascinated by this unknown shore and the mystery of what lay beyond. Though he had had to turn back because the codfish were smaller and poorer, the north still called. If the King should support the project, Louis would like nothing better than to try it again.

No one had ever mapped the grim, dangerous Labrador
coast, and more and more trading was heading in that direction; more and more the English and French were dis-
puting the sea rights to Hudson Bay and the trading there.
A good map of the coast would be an invaluable aid and
advantage to the French, for the English evidently did not
have one.

Jolliet sent a long letter to M. Lagny, on November 2,
1693:

Sir:
   As soon as I heard that you wished to have one of my
maps, I set to work with all possible zeal and diligence to
satisfy your wish. In the past eighteen years I have navigated
the whole of the St. Lawrence River several times; I have
noted the bearings from one point to another, and have taken
and kept a record of latitudes of many landmarks. Hudson
Strait on this map is based on very accurate memoires which
M. Iberville gave me.
   You will not find on my map "the passage of Canceau,"
nor is Placentia inscribed on it, because I was never there,
and I prefer for the present to send you an incomplete rather
than a defective map.
   I only went within five or six days' sailing of that sea
which I call "unknown" at latitude 57 degrees, 30 minutes
[Ungava Bay]. However, the Indians whom I met on the
way assured me that it is a large sea, that the water extends
indefinitely toward the north. This makes me think that the
whole coast line that borders on Hudson Strait is just a series
of islands, and that other passages by which to enter the bay
could be found which are not so far north, and consequently
off the route of our enemies.
   Had it not been for the two serious losses inflicted on me
by the English, I would have followed up this discovery, but
unless the Court gives me some assistance, it is useless for
me to think of it. You are all powerful, Sir, and I have no
doubt that if the King wishes this discovery to be followed
up, you will one day experience the joy of having been the

first to make known to those barbarians the light of the Gospel and the knowledge of His Majesty's magnificence. We might be able to carry on a rather heavy trade with them in seal and whale oil, and defray part of the expenses by catching codfish on the way to their country.

If I am considered to accomplish this enterprise, I will continually hold myself in readiness to undertake it promptly and to be faithful in my service.

With all humility, I beg of you, Sir, to present my petition to my Lord de Pontchartrain, and to remember what M. the Count de Frontenac is writing to you in my behalf. I will be infinitely obliged for the favors, yet they will not make me to be more completely than I now am, Sir, your most humble and obedient servant,

JOLLIET

To this letter Frontenac, who had liked and admired Jolliet for some time, his earlier antipathy having worn off in spite of himself, added a footnote to Lagny, saying:

He sustained a serious loss three years ago when the English came to attack us. They seized his bark, his wife, his mother-in-law and goods worth more than ten or twelve thousand francs. Last year two English ships consummated his ruin:—all the buildings at Mingan and Seven Islands were burnt down, and all that was left to him carried away.

And again Frontenac added another note to the letter:

Jolliet takes the liberty of sending a petition. He is clever, intelligent, and able to acquit himself successfully of any undertaking entrusted to him.

Evidently, then, with these enthusiastic recommendations, the King sent word for Jolliet to proceed with his plans. Louis, however, had to finance the Labrador trip himself. To do this, he persuaded a merchant, M. François-Vianney Pachot, to provide ship and gear, to be repaid by profits from the voyage, mainly from cod caught en route. Louis was to make the map of the Labrador coast, and he probably expected to be paid for it. His Majesty was a difficult man to persuade to invest money in any doubtful undertaking, any intangible substance; but usually he saw the light after the thing was done, if successful, and he paid handsomely, either in land grants or in cash.

The *St. François* was ready and loaded by noon on April 28, 1694. There were the usual delays, however, so it was not until three in the afternoon that the anchor was weighed. As the sails filled, the ship moved slowly away from the harbor of Québec and down the misty, cold waters of the St. Lawrence.

April on this northern river was still almost winter. There were great banks of old snow, dirtied by winter smokes, along the back streets of the city. Out in the spruce forests the snow was still deep and fresh; it had the look of lasting forever. Spring was indeed coming, but in all that Canadian country only the blossoming of the first arbutus on sunny south banks and the voices of migrant birds in the night could indicate its nearness with any surety.

The snow geese were back in a great white flock drifting on the dark waters at the mouth of the Saguenay, but they would have to wait before going on to their nesting places in the hidden north. Louis, like the geese, knew spring was coming, knew that when it reached the St. Lawrence and the silent Saguenay it would still have a long way to go before it attained the upper country and the tundra, before it would open the ice pack around Labrador, would move out the ice so that his ship could enter without being crushed in a great squeeze on a freezing night. He wanted to time his voyage so that all that menace of winter was past; yet, to be early enough to carry out his exploration of this hitherto unmapped, rugged coast and get out before the early winter closed in. A ship caught in the Labrador ice pack early in the season might have to stay there all winter.

Although the entire Jolliet family had, for years, sailed down this river bound for a summer at Mingan or Anticosti, there was a greater air of excitement on that April day as the *St. François* set sail. Again the whole family was aboard, but Louis intended to leave his wife and three youngest children at Mingan until his return in the fall. This time, however, he was going to take along with him his three big sons—Louis, who was eighteen now and had left the seminary after his classical education was completed; Charles, who was sixteen, and François, fifteen. They were well-grown, intelligent, well-educated, enthusiastic youths, and they were wonderfully excited to have the chance to go along with their famous father on a voyage of discovery. They had gone out for codfish with him, of course, but that was work, not adventure. To explore the land of the strange people called the Eskimo, to see new coasts, to help map an unknown part of the globe—they could hardly wait for the departure, and were all over the ship at once, their father complained, yet never in sight when he needed a hand.

Louis was preoccupied with the poor quality of the cable on one anchor. It didn't look new or strong to him, but M. Pachot had bought his gear from a reliable chandler and insisted that he had paid a good price for the cable, so it must be all right. Louis was still doubtful. He couldn't be sure about the cable until they tried it out. He didn't like going off half equipped or with goods of dubious quality. Neither the wilderness nor the sea was the place to discover that one had been fleeced or had made a mistake in judgment.

Before he could decide whether he would send the cable

back and demand another, or take a chance on what he had, Claire-Françoise had bustled aboard with the three youngest children, Jean-Baptiste, aged eleven, Marie-Geneviève, thirteen, and Claire, nine. Not present was Marie Lalande, who had spent the winter with her husband and two other Frenchmen at Mingan. Though the buildings there had been destroyed by the English, Marie had sturdily insisted that they should rebuild what they could before winter; and, if nothing better offered, they would live like Indians in a bark hut until spring.

If the Mingan settlement was totally deserted, there was no knowing, with so many scoundrels about, who might come in and destroy the little that remained, or decide to take over the place. Also, if the men were left there alone, Mme Lalande insisted, they would do nothing. With her there to supervise, what wonders could they not accomplish!

Jean-Baptiste did not want to be left at Mingan with his mother, sisters, and grandmother. He felt that he was old enough to go with his older brothers. To have to stay behind was something of a disgrace in his eyes, marking him plainly as a baby and not yet in the enviable category of men to which Louis, Charles, and François obviously had come. But Louis Jolliet only shook his head when the boy pleaded and coaxed, trying some new tack to persuade his obdurate parent to take him along. Jean-Baptiste was not old enough; he would have to stay and help take care of his sisters.

The *St. François*, sailing into the opalescent mists of afternoon that suffused the St. Lawrence and the dimming form of the city on the rock and the lower town with its smokes and masts and busy life, was well loaded. She carried six guns called *pierriers*, whose cannon balls were made of stone, and fourteen other guns, and a supply of ammunition. The crew numbered eighteen, according to Jolliet's report, including three cadets and a Récollet Father whose name

Jolliet never gave in his journal. He did not name the cadets: they might have been his own sons, Louis, Charles, and François.

By the first day of May they were sailing past Matane on the south shore of the Gaspé, where there usually is a tricky northwest wind to combat, and as the winds increased, they finally had to anchor off Egg Island on the third day. The west side of the island formed an excellent shelter. It was so incessantly windy and the Gulf of St. Lawrence was so disturbed, they had to stay at Egg Island four days, while the wind gusted wildly about and Louis chafed at the enforced delay. Then the weather suddenly changed and snow started to fall.

The south wind, filled with warm moisture, now met the colder air of the Gaspé—and the gulf, the rocky island, and the ship were all swallowed in a tumultuous smothering whiteness that came horizontally with flakes as big as butterflies, wet and heavy and fierce, hurled at the ship with great force. Then it stopped as abruptly as it began, but by the time the crew was out sweeping the heavy snow off the decks, the flakes began again, intermittently in an overwhelming spring blizzard or in sudden quiet emptiness.

The storm continued all night. Snow was heaped in drifts on the decks by morning. The wind, which had changed again, came chill and fresh from the northwest. The clouds blew off and a bright sky, cold and polished and exhilarating with sunshine, arched above the glittering water.

They had just shoveled the snow off the decks and shaken out the furled sails and weighed anchor, when the cable, the one which Louis had suspected before they sailed from Québec, snapped. The anchor vanished irretrievably into the depths of the St. Lawrence.

It was a poor beginning for a long trip. Louis was a good deal exasperated by his own inefficiency in not doing something about the weakened rope when he had had the chance, but there was nothing to do about it now, and they did have two other anchors. The ship proceeded to Mingan, on the north shore of the Gulf of St. Lawrence, on the eleventh day of May, where Claire's baggage and food supplies were unloaded. Everyone went ashore. Tools and equipment had been brought to rebuild and refurnish the burned buildings and there was much work to be done.

Marie and Claire-Françoise rushed to meet each other. They embraced with tears and kisses and laughter, and then Marie hugged her grandchildren in turn, starting with little Claire and standing on tiptoe to kiss big Louis, who had to obligingly bend over for his grandmother's affectionate greeting. The winter had been so long that Marie, as the only woman here, had found it unbearably dull, with only a few Indians coming to trade, the men to be urged incessantly to work, and the endless snows piling up. The ice lying in a vast dazzle across the St. Lawrence had been so bright it had hurt her eyes.

The big boys didn't care for the idea of staying at Mingan for a while, or of being expected to work so hard. They would have preferred to go on at once to adventure, but their father assured them that even if they did go on, they couldn't get through the ice packs. They were much too early for that, but not too early to bend their backs and to hammer pegs and do the work that was needful here.

The trading post was soon rebuilt on the west side of the mouth of the Mingan River. Indians were coming regularly with pelts and dried meat. Everyone was very busy. Louis kept a weather eye on the height of the sun, on the direction of the wind, on the coming of June. All the geese had long since passed over, had left the Saguenay and were hidden in the north. If the geese found it favorable for nesting and the laying of eggs on the tundra, then the snow must be largely gone, the pools open, the sea emptying itself of ice. It was time to be on their way with the *St. François*.

On June 9 they went aboard, leaving behind four of the men and Michel De Sorcis, the young manservant who was by now indistinguishably a part of the family. Claire-Françoise relied upon Michel to do many of the things which her husband would have done if he were at home. She could count on Michel, and he repaid with a devotion which, at times, might have seemed greater even than that which her sons gave her.

The sails filled, Louis and the others were aboard, and the little group on the wooden landing at Mingan waved. Louis could see that Claire-Françoise put her handkerchief to her eyes, and then shook it aloft energetically before applying it again. Michel was standing close beside her. Louis could hear little Claire's high voice crying her farewells.

Then they could no longer hear the voices, could only see the flash of the white handkerchief and the indistinctness of the group. There was always that solemn thought beneath the farewells: Would he ever come back? Would he ever see his beloved family again? There was always that wrench at his heart in parting; yet, once out of sight, he always seemed to be able to leave worries behind and to anticipate only the things which might lie ahead.

They had gone on, after all, without having done anything about a new sheet cable and a new anchor. They had debated while at Mingan whether they should send back to Québec for new equipment. Somewhat against his better judgment, at the last, Louis had decided that they would go on with the other two anchors. But he was sorry for M. François-Vianney Pachot, the owner of the ship, who had spared no expense to equip it, and now had obviously been cheated. Cables, Louis mused bitterly, rot away more quickly in an attic than on the high sea.

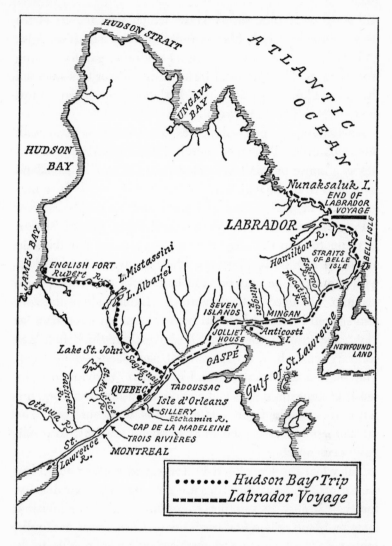

The dramatic coastline along the Côte Nord was rugged and dark, with cliffs of red-brown rock sloping down to the sea. On all the ledges and islands the sea birds roosted or were beginning to nest—black sea-pigeons and gaudy-beaked puffins which plummeted across the bow of the ship, back and forth as if they didn't know which way to go. There were murres in sleek black-and-white rows on the ledges, gulls keening past and coasting on updrafts, gannets diving from heights. The clamor of birds as the ship at times neared the sheer cliffs or bird-whitened islands became an almost deafening racket and turmoil of wings.

Navigation was often difficult. The water was filled with hundreds of small islands, merely jagged chunks of rock as big as a house or small as a dory, or forming a larger island separated from the mainland rocks themselves only by a narrow *rigole* or pass.

Progress was slow, and not only because of the islands. In order to map the coastline it was necessary for the ship to put in at mouths of rivers while Louis got his bearings with the astrolabe and put the landmarks and readings on his map. The need to trade with any Indians along the way also slowed them, and so did having to avoid navigation at night, because of the rocks. Bad weather, thick fog, and contrary winds held up the ship at one place after another. The Indians at Mekattina and elsewhere, oblivious to any sense of time or urgency, haggled lengthily over their inferior furs, while Louis chafed at the waste of time. The northern summer was too short to spend any of it so prodigally over nothing.

But when the fog closed in, there was nothing to do but wait it out. St. Lawrence fogs are notorious for their density, for their ability to smother everything and make invisible even an island only a few yards away. Cormorants and gulls, fog-pearled, sat on their wave-splashed rocks, unable to fly very far. Ducks lost their way. The puffins hurtled past, however, and vanished in the fog. Little black-and-white Labrador ducks bobbed on the water in sheltered coves and did not venture beyond. The sulphurous smell of the kelp lying limp on the rocks at low tide was an unmistakable indication to Louis that the ship was too close to shore, and he would move outward a distance for greater safety.

In order to avoid the rocky islands, Jolliet usually kept well offshore in the enclosing white murk, but even on the thickest days he managed to proceed, though only at a crawl. The ship moved up into the narrower straits. When the fog at last cleared and there was a splendid sunset spreading its gold over the waters, Louis discovered on his right a dim, rock-bound, tree-capped mass on the horizon. It was Newfoundland.

On this day and on those which followed, Jolliet began to note that the codfish became smaller, though they were still fairly abundant. He was puzzled by this. He had noted the same thing on his earlier venture up along these shores. Evidently the finicky cod preferred a more southern sea, yet not too far south, either.

The *St. François* moved into the narrowing reaches of the Straits of Belle Isle between Newfoundland and the curve of the Labrador coast, and out to the Atlantic Ocean at last.

On July 11, they were in the open sea. And far across the heaving gray-blue expanse of ocean that morning they discovered strange white shapes moving along the horizon. They were like huge, ghostly ships lit blue-white and marked with deep cobalt shadows against the sky. Louis watched in fascination; the boys joined him, asking questions. As the shapes came a little closer, Louis, with a twinge of awe and alarm, knew that they were massive icebergs. He had seen small remnants of icebergs before, but nothing at all so huge, not even when he was at Hudson Bay when they had lain on the far horizon and he could not judge how large they really were. But these were truly enormous.

As if drawn to them, the little ship moved closer and with some difficulty was diverted from its strange and dangerous affinity for the ice. If the ship was in iceberg waters, then

Louis and the crew must be doubly watchful, for these were dangerous for a vessel to meet unexpectedly, and certainly to be avoided at night or in fog. He would have to post a special watch and could never dare to sail in darkness. He knew that more than three-fourths of an iceberg lay beneath the water, and that often there were great jagged portions extending outward underwater so that a ship approaching too close would be totally wrecked and lost. He had heard sailors say that they could "smell" an iceberg when it was close; that it had a certain kind of damp, chill breath which revealed its presence, but Louis knew he must not count on that.

He watched, and the crew watched, while the three Jolliet boys, hanging on the rail, stared at the eerie, castlelike bergs, bigger than a dozen ships together, slowly going by.

To be out of the way of passing ice during the night, they prudently anchored the *St. François* among the barren, lichen-covered islands opposite the Labrador coast. At dawn they were set back on their heels by two explosions, like cannon shots, only greater and with more echoes than any cannon. Louis tumbled from his bunk, threw on his clothes, and was out on deck in a hurry, the men following.

There should have been no cannon in these waters. No ship was in sight, and there was no sign of habitation on the islands, no telltale puff of smoke to show where the explosions originated, only that great booming thunder, and then a silence which seemed almost as loud and ominous in its implications.

Louis was alarmed. He was on a peaceful expedition; and though the ship carried guns, he and his crew were certainly not equipped for war and could ill afford to get into trouble with strangers. It must be the English. He had heard strange legends of a mysterious fort and colony on the Labrador coast, but he could see no sign of anything there, only the dark, curving contours of the mountains, the low green arctic spruces, the sea-birds flying.

He took two of his men and went out in a canoe to investigate around the island and into the coves on the mainland. Quietly they paddled around the island and examined the bare, red-brown, towering headlands. They saw no one. Mainland and island lay silent and unspeaking in the cosmic stillness of the north.

Then as they paddled around to the seaward side, they suddenly saw two enormous icebergs bearing down on them from the northeast, not so very far away and dark gray and sullen in the morning mist, truly mountainous, terrifying, and unbelievably massive. They were particularly ugly and awe-inspiring as seen from the low point of a canoe at water level. Kittiwakes and puffins were riding along on one of the ice masses, when suddenly another tremendous explosion shook the air, the sea, and the ship. The birds screeched and swirled into the air as one of the icebergs split apart, rent in two as by a giant ax. Pieces hit the water in a great splash as high as the ship and bobbed to the surface again. Broken ice surged all about. The waves rocked the ship and sent the canoe up and down on giant swells which thundered in sudden breakers on the island and the mainland.

When the tumult in the water subsided, Louis and his companions began to laugh, though a trifle weakly. They paddled hastily back to the ship. Those aboard who had witnessed the breaking up of the iceberg were shaken. What tremendous power in that ice-thing, what horror if the ship had been too close! The whole experience had had an almost supernatural quality. Afterward, the great silence was almost oppressive.

To give the ice time to go by, Louis decided to land in the cove which he had seen and admired as they paddled by in the canoe. He had thought that he glimpsed a sort of house, and yet could not be sure.

An Eskimo dwelling of sticks, rocks, and mud was set in a little cove in front of three rocky hills, snow still deep in their sheltered ravines. Beyond lay a magnificent sea view. Evidently some twenty people and many dogs had spent several winters in this place, yet no living person was in sight, and no live animals, either. Wildflowers and low grass grew from the mud roof, and all around the house Louis found chunks of fat from recently killed seals. The place smelled of putrid meat and it was well to be on the lee side of it.

Louis had hoped that ashore they might find some kind of game, for meat was scarce aboard, and the men were growing tired of fish. But it was a desolate land, as if all life had departed.

The men had gone back aboard and, after a final survey of the place, Louis was about to leave, when something made him turn his head and he paused, transfixed and almost unbelieving. The men saw it, too, at that same moment. A caribou! A live caribou! Unconcerned, it came walking along on its big hairy feet over the rocks and lichens, bending its head to nip bites of moss.

With one shot, Louis dropped the animal, and the men were ashore with their knives almost before it had died. They were in such haste to cut up the meat that, as Louis wrote in his journal, . . . "a caribou came along to make us a present of its hide and meat. If our men had not been in such a hurry we would have had both, as well as its fine, large antlers."

But the men were too hungry, and, although they took the antlers, they slashed the skin beyond any hope of saving. They only had one thought—to carve out steaks and roasts in a trice, leaving the bloody remains for the ravens and gulls to finish, and hurrying with the meat to the ship's galley. Dinner that night was a succulent one aboard the *St. François*. Louis fastened up the caribou's antlers on the mast. He would take them home to Jean-Baptiste, who had never seen this sort of animal on which they had thankfully dined.

The ship proceeded ever northward. It was beset with strong winds and again and again had to seek shelter behind islands or in beautiful bays. Louis meanwhile carefully mapped the area. He was disappointed, however, in not having seen any Eskimos. He was certain that they lived here.

On July 14 the sea was in such a tumult that he stayed in a bay until next day. Two hours after they set sail, Louis Jolliet saw his first Eskimos.

The two were in sealskin canoes, kayaks (though Louis did not know the word), curious craft which were new to him. The kayak lay so low in the water, was so trim and narrow and appeared to be so dangerous, if mishandled, he could not understand how the Eskimos could stay upright on the heaving sea. They seemed highly proficient, however, their double-bladed paddles twirling so fast that the little boats skimmed over the water and almost up to the ship. The two Eskimos had some pelts to trade, but refused to come aboard or paddle any closer.

Over and over again they shouted words which Louis hastily wrote in his journal: *"Ahé, ahé, thou, tcharacou!"*

He didn't know what the men were trying to say to him, but could see they were beckoning. Three of his men went with him in the ship's launch, with some knives for trading, to meet the two Eskimos in the bobbing kayaks.

19

~~~~~~

ESKIMO COUNTRY

LOUIS WAS EXCITED to be face to face with Eskimos at last.
When he and his men with the launch caught up with the
bobbing kayaks, he discovered that one Eskimo was an old
man with a dense and very black beard no more than a
quarter of an inch long, as if he had simply neglected to
shave for a week. This one pointed to himself and indicated
that he was, as Louis understood it, called Capitena Ioannis.
The other was smooth-faced; his name was Kamicterineac.
Both were large men, fat and tall, though it was hard to be
sure just how large they really were, since they were compressed in the kayaks. Both had surprisingly light skins. Jolliet had once pictured the Eskimos as dark like the Indians
of the interior. These were a different sort of people, definitely not Indians, either in skin color or in physical appearance and character.

With gestures and smiles, the two invited Louis and his
men to follow them to shore. As Jolliet wrote later in his
journal: "They invited us to come and anchor in a nearby
cove. We could do our trading there, they said, and bivouac
together; they would provide girls to entertain us during the
night. This was their way of letting us know that *tcharacou,*
that is, peace, prevailed everywhere."

He ended laconically: "We let it go at that."

Louis was, in fact, not too eager to go ashore just then. He had no idea how honest these two Eskimos were, nor how many others might be hiding behind the rocks, waiting to attack when the French came close enough. So he explained with signs and words that they would come back tomorrow—tomorrow morning—and Capitena Ioannis and the greasy-faced Kamicterineac nodded and smiled. Then they paddled quickly to the shore and were suddenly out of sight around a rocky headland. Louis and his men returned to the ship.

He decided that since he wanted to learn more about the Eskimos, the way to do so was to risk the chance of ambush. He sailed the ship into the harbor, forthwith christening the place and adding it to the map as St. François Bay, after the ship, and in honor of Sieur François-Vianney Pachot, who had provided everything for the journey, and without whom no doubt they would not have been here.

It was too late to go ashore then. They kept a good watch during the night, and about eight o'clock next morning, on the sixteenth of July, the same two men came out on the hill above the bay, waved their arms, and shouted: *"Ahé, ahé!"*

Louis would have much preferred to entice them aboard. He felt safer if they were with him, rather than if he were at their mercy on the unknown shore. But they were obviously afraid of setting foot on the ship, so Jolliet and four of his men rowed ashore. The Eskimos came forward then, massive men in their fur garments, tailed parka hoods, and stout sealskin boots, still saying: *"Ahé, ahé, thou, tcharacou!"* in loud voices, repeating the last word over and over. Jolliet decided that they meant: "Lay down the arms, no treachery!"

Setting the example, then, the Eskimos put their bows and arrows as well as a gun on the ground while they were still at a distance from the French. They signaled to Louis and the men to do the same, which they did in the boat, though the crewmen did so with some misgiving. Jolliet knew, however, that the rest of his men and his sons were covering the entire operation from the ship.

As soon as Louis climbed on to the rocks, the Eskimos looked astonished and immediately retreated. From farther away, they signaled for Louis to get back into the boat, which he did. This trading expedition was turning into a farce if neither side could get close enough to do business with the other.

Then the two worried natives smiled again and said, *"Catchia!"* which Louis decided must mean "that's good," and their faces beamed with relief. The situation was growing funny.

Finally, however, the pair got enough courage to come and trade. One, however, always stood close to the bows and arrows lying on the ground, while the other did the bartering.

Louis wrote down several words of the new language and their meanings, as he understood them, and asked the men for more. The Eskimos, obviously pleased, flattered, and surprised, obliged. But in spite of feeling that he had gained their confidence, Louis was disappointed when the two, the meager trading finished, told the Frenchmen to go back to the ship. Humoring them, Louis did, and was somewhat disconcerted to see the two get into their kayaks and set off up the coast without even a backward look. Louis waited until next day; and when there was no sign of the two timid Eskimos, he weighed anchor and departed from that place.

After five days of pleasant, uneventful sailing along the rocky, much indented Labrador coast, many hours occupied in careful drawing on the map and in taking the sun's height, naming capes and headlands and bays, they arrived beyond the St. Thomas Islands, grim and wind-whipped and wave-lashed, full of gulls and cormorants. Louis landed on one of the islands and climbed to the top of the rocks to survey the scene.

The wind whipped him and tossed his hair, filling him with an excitement and buoyancy. He shielded his eyes from the glare of the sun, scanning the sea for any sign of Eskimo boats, and the shores for any sign of huts, but he saw nothing. He had wanted to send up smoke signals, but on this barren island there were only caribou moss and scrub willows three inches high; there was neither wood nor peat to make a fire. No wonder there were no people about.

This great loneliness of the north was an almost tangible thing. Although he had known how it was on the tundra when he went to Hudson Bay, that was as a full symphony as compared with the silent desolation of this coast and this sea. But more than the emptiness, it was the absence of Eskimos which disturbed Louis. It was not only to map the coast but also to learn about the people that he had come. The date was July 22, and he could stay in the north no later than mid-August if he expected to get out before winter closed in and the ice came.

But it was on that day that the ship suddenly bore down on a group of Eskimos in kayaks, who fled in their boats to hide behind an island. They landed there, and then, summoning courage, waved sealskins and shouted the usual *"Ahé, ahé!"*

Six men, each in his kayak, finally ventured to the ship where they made bold to come close enough to trade a few skins. They waved their hands and gestured to Louis to sail into the bay which lay ahead, and they would follow to lead the way to their village where trading would be very much better than this. The sealskins brought to the ship were full of holes and looked as if cats had been fighting over them.

The ship went considerably faster than the kayaks, for the wind was good; and, as he was rapidly outdistancing them, he ordered the sails clewed up and waited for the kayaks manned by the red-faced and breathless Eskimos to take the lead. Four leagues up the channel lay the village.

That afternoon the *St. François* anchored off the village where Louis counted nearly a dozen lodges. Nine men came out to signal and harangue. They traded and went back, apparently very happy. But soon afterward Louis saw smoke signals rising from the top of the hill; he wondered what they meant. Two kayaks, meanwhile, came out, one bearing the chief himself, an imposing individual named Quignac who was distinguished by a large black mustachio curled up in the Spanish style and of noble proportions.

He evidently had intended to come straight out to the ship, but his timorous men were appalled by such rashness and called him back for a conference. Louis wished he knew what they were saying with such elaborate gestures. But evidently Quignac was not intimidated. He ordered the village to turn out to greet the guests; and, following the chief's kayak, there came ten more in line, all the men dipping their paddles in unison and chanting, *"Tcharacou, tcharacou"*—"Peace to all, peace everywhere, lay down arms, no treachery, good captains!"

Louis went out in the launch to meet the procession. He was greeted with a cordial embrace from kayak to launch which threatened to pitch him and Quignac precipitously into the sea. Then the chief got down to business and traded some wrapped-up items he had on hand for some knives from Jolliet. Louis, out of curiosity, took what the chief gave him. When the Eskimos had gone back to shore and had promised to come tomorrow with more trade items, Louis, back on the ship, examined what Quignac had given him. He unwrapped the tattered sealskin. The boys gathered around in excitement.

Then Louis began to laugh. The farther he unwrapped the packet the funnier the whole situation became, and the boys joined him in amusement. Here were primitive people, Eskimos, and what had they given him, the visiting Frenchman from the land of civilization?

A brand-new white shirt, a colored linen handkerchief, a sack in which were a few pages from a Spanish book which had some passages from the *Acts of the Apostles* written in the margin, in Spanish; and some remnants of linen belts and bags—these were the gifts.

Evidently the amiable Quignac and his band had been preying upon Spanish fishing vessels that sometimes, Louis had heard, came into the northern waters. Well, he himself would have to be on his guard.

Early the next morning the Eskimos were back. There was a little trading done, of small value, but Louis collected more words of the Eskimo tongue for his journal. The men were cheerful, affable, and inclined to laugh, and this pleased Louis, who always loved a good joke and a good laugh. When the Eskimos invited Jolliet and his men to come and visit the village, he accepted, even though his distrust of Quignac was still evident. He would take the chance of ambush.

That night he saw fires on the headlands and smoke rising to the sky. He kept a watch all night, but nothing happened. There was only the eerie flaring of the aurora borealis reflecting itself in the sea and illuminating with a pallid glow the headlands and shores.

Next morning he went ashore with some of his men, where he was greeted with shouts of joy from the people, the usual protestation of "Peace, peace, peace," and the promises of wonderful trading to be done.

The round-faced, solemn, black-eyed Eskimo children stared at the newcomers. The women, whom Louis admired because they were so pretty and modest and neat, gathered around, giggling to each other and watching the visitors. Quignac clapped his hands and ordered some of the women to sing for the visitors, and they gathered in a group to comply. Louis liked what he heard. As a musician he could appreciate good voices, and these were well modulated and sweet. This was followed by a long dance performed by the women, who still sang in a rhythmic cadence to the beat of their booted feet.

Then the French, not to be outdone by the musical talents of the Eskimos, put on a show for their hosts. There was a demonstration of a French chant, led by Louis Jolliet and the Reverend Recollect Father. Then the father intoned the *Sub tuum*, and the *Domine salvum*, which was followed and considerably lightened by a rollicking rendition of a French folk song and some of the boisterous songs of the *coureurs des bois*. And the Eskimos listened at first with awe at the solemn music, then beamed and laughed and clapped when the music grew happier. It was altogether a very pleasant occasion.

This took place about eight o'clock in the morning, however, and after that nothing more happened. The Frenchmen went back to the ship. After dinner, growing impatient with all the fruitless waiting, the Reverend Recollect Father, young François Jolliet, and five of the men decided to stop dawdling around. They would go ashore and visit the Eskimos. Anything was better than sitting around with nothing to do.

As if he had been expecting them, Chief Quignac came out in his kayak to meet them. He showed them the best place to land the launch, only a short distance from the houses, and assisted the priest to shore. Taking him firmly

by the hand, Quignac led him with a good deal of elaborate
ceremony around the village. The men remained with their
guns ready in the launch, but were far from ignored. All the
young people in the village came and crowded about to
look at them. The people made comments to each other, all
very solemnly until someone burst into a laugh. Then they
all laughed, and young François wanted to laugh, too, but
he didn't know what the joke was. Then he began to suspect
that it might be he himself they were laughing at, so he
scowled terribly, and at this the Eskimo children laughed
all the harder.

The priest was taken to the chief's house, where the
latter's wife met them and took some pride in showing the
guest the establishment. Quignac still held the priest by
the hand, and when they proceeded into the other houses,
he maintained a firm grip on the father's perspiring palm.
In each cabin, the Reverend Recollect Father was given
refreshments of not very good seal meat—when properly
cooked it tasted like good roast beef, but this was not well
cooked—and seal oil, evidently the best food they had to
offer. Before he had concluded his visit, the Reverend Recollect Father was somewhat greasy of mouth and unwilling
to think of any kind of food for some time.

The next day, Louis with eight armed men went to visit
the chief. Quignac, the great black mustache fairly quiver-
ing with enthusiasm, engulfed Louis in a mammoth embrace
and kissed him, took him by the hand, and proceeded to
his house. The chief's elderly wife immediately kissed him,
French-fashion. So did Quignac's married daughter and her
husband. Louis responded; it was evidently considered to
be a token of friendship and politeness, though it had rather
surprised him.

He admitted later, however, that there was really nothing

at all unpleasant in these manifestations of esteem. Unlike many Indians he had known, these people were clean, and their skins pleasant to the touch.

He was also impressed with the cleanliness of the houses, as well as the universal politeness wherever he went. The chief, with great tact, nonetheless brought shame upon one of the Frenchmen, Denis de la Ferté. The latter had heard the fable that Eskimos drank salt water, and he decided to find out for himself whether or not this were true. There was a skin bucket of water in a house. He rudely dipped his hand into it to taste the water.

Quignac saw him do it. He quickly asked the woman of the house to give the guest a cup because he was thirsty. Denis flushed. As a visitor in a French home, he suddenly recalled with shame, he would never have dipped his hand into a pitcher of water. He apologized to the woman and to the chief, but there was little he could do to erase the impression of boorishness which he must have given to the Eskimos.

The visiting was well enough; it was interesting, though often rather tiresome. Louis was learning some facts about the Eskimos which might be of value. But the people were bringing forth no good sealskins to trade. There was little purpose in staying, though Quignac urged them to wait longer; he was certain that some other Eskimos would soon be arriving with some really fine trade items.

Nevertheless, Jolliet planned to leave next day. That night there was a wild storm with heavy rain followed by thick fog. On July 26, they could do nothing but sit tight and wait. The following night was increasingly nasty. It rained in sheets; and the wind blew, shifting from the southwest to the north and then northwest, and turning so cold ultimately that there was a glitter of ice on a water bucket next morning. It was a warning. He could not stay very much longer in the land of the Eskimo.

Before turning south, he wanted to go a little farther north along the coast. Though winds still harassed him, Jolliet made his farewells to Quignac and his people. On August 4 they found a beautiful bay, island-studded, with a great purple mountain at the end. He named the place Pachot Bay for the ship's owner. The ceremony of naming the bay was no sooner completed and Mass said, when Eskimos suddenly appeared. Headed by a chief named Alienak, a fleet of more than a dozen kayaks bobbed on the water around the ship. There were men, women, even children, all staring at this wonderful craft and offering small trade items. They had little that Jolliet wanted and he had no time to dally. As quickly as he could he went on, then lost a good deal of time when they grounded between two islands. When the tide finally rose to float the ship again, they headed for the safety of the open sea.

On the ninth, when he went ashore to take the altitude of the sun, he discovered, across from where he computed the latitude, a great bay whose end he could not see, any more than he could see the end of Pachot Bay. He wondered about it. He had found so many of these long clefts in the rocky shoreline of Labrador, these long bays whose end he never saw or had the time to explore, and each one was a challenge. If he only had the time and could stay away from his business; if he could devote the rest of his life to finding out where the long bays led, to see what lay beyond the next mountain, and the next island, and discover where the rivers went. If he only could!

Time was running out, yet a sea wind prevented their getting up sail until August 11. Then, just as they were taking up the anchor and unfurling the sails, three kayaks commanded by the same Eskimo they had met some days earlier, Alienak, came hastily with twirling paddles out to the ship. Alienak, apparently, was very angry about something, and finally, as his fury mounted, and he gestured and shouted and pointed at the sails which the men were lifting, Louis decided that the chief didn't want them to leave. He had just caught up with the ship again, and now it was about to go on before he and his people had had time to trade. To humor him, Jolliet ordered the sails down and the anchors dropped.

As if at a signal, a swarm of kayaks bustled out from shore. The people did a little nondescript trading, and then returned to shore for the night. As soon as daylight came, a fleet of no less than twenty-two kayaks appeared, together with three larger boats bearing skin sails. These vessels were heavily loaded with women, girls, and boys of all ages and assorted sizes, young and old, short and tall. They also wanted to trade their few sealskins and to sing their songs. The women seldom had a chance to trade for things they needed, and now here they were without the men, obviously delighted. Some came up on the ship itself. They were not at all afraid, as the men apparently were at first.

The Reverend Recollect Father was amused by them. Whereupon, some of the women invited him to come to one of their boats to see the children and old women who had remained on board. Without any misgivings and only pleased that he might possibly have a chance to minister to some unregenerate souls, the Recollect Father went with the women and boarded one of the boats. He gave small presents to the women and children, and said a prayer and blessed them.

Jolliet, watching from the *St. François,* hadn't been so pleased by anything for a long time. He called to Louis, François, and Charles, and to Denis de la Ferté and the others. They hung over the railing, laughing. For the Reverend Recollect Father was being mobbed by the ladies. Some embraced him from both sides at once, and a few old women rushed at him with open mouths, then clacked their snaggy teeth in his face, while he ducked and dodged—and they, laughing shrilly, closed in and kissed him solidly and wetly.

Louis laughed until the tears came as the women so surrounded the father that he couldn't be seen, until he emerged, flushed and rumpled, and with mounting determination to get off the Eskimo ship as fast as possible. He called to Louis for help, but Jolliet only waved at him and continued to laugh. The priest was a large, burly fellow and certainly could take care of himself.

It was plain that the women didn't want him to go. Shrieking, they pretended to hold him so he couldn't move, and an old woman approached, again clacking her discolored teeth at him to within an inch of his nose, and then gave him an enthusiastic kiss on the cheek, and still another, while the girls screamed in delight.

The priest gave up trying to change the subject by praying. With feeling in his voice and a reproachful glance across at the heartless Jolliet, he kept saying *"Tcharacou, tcharacou,"* and moved firmly toward the edge of the boat. He flopped over the side into the launch, making it rock furiously, and the sailor waiting for him paddled back to the safety of the ship. The Reverend Recollect Father showed no further interest in going back to visit the Eskimos or preach to them. Clearly, he had had enough.

Jolliet invited Amaillouk, one of the chiefs, aboard. He was a swarthy individual whose black brows met over his nose. With him was a younger man who, while Jolliet was engaged in trying to talk to Amaillouk in the cabin, contrived to steal Jolliet's compass.

Louis hadn't seen the theft or he would have halted the

thief at once. The young man hastily went back to his canoe and slipped the compass to his wife, but someone saw her hiding it inside her boot. Word reached Louis. Hastily checking, he discovered with anger that the compass was indeed missing. It was a costly one, and he needed it. He didn't like to incur the wrath of the natives, but he wanted what was rightfully his, so he ordered the woman sent for. She came, kicking and biting and struggling between two sailors who were laughing at her futile efforts to get away. She was a large, stout, strong woman and the two men were having to use all their strength to hold her.

Louis demanded the compass. She refused, with insolence, and spat at him.

"Search her, then," commanded Jolliet.

The woman bent quickly to try to hide the compass between her thighs, but the sailors were too quick for her, and one of them caught her fat hand and squeezed it until she gave up. Louis leaped to retrieve the instrument before it fell on the floor.

But, to the Eskimo woman, worse than having had to give up the compass was the detestable fact that Louis and the others were laughing at her. The more they laughed, the more angry she became. The sight of Louis Jolliet standing there, hands on lean hips, looking down and laughing at her, a fat, furious female, suddenly changed her mood again. Her own Eskimo love of a joke struggled with her anger at being circumvented. Her round face was a momentary tumult between wrath and amusement, and suddenly she shrieked in a great burst of laughter. And the sailors roared, and so did Louis, and the whole thing ended in fun.

Louis knew they must leave. He named the bay Ste Claire, because it was her feast day, but it was really named for his wife and for his youngest daughter, both of whom he longed to see. But the wind fell just as they were ready to go, and so, in spite of himself, Louis had to drop anchor once again. He was worried. His anchor cables were growing too weak and worn to last safely in any severe storms; he only hoped they would endure through the coming weather on the long route home.

Summer was already breathing into autumn, and heavy autumn winds and rains were at hand. The ship must turn about at this point, at about 57 degrees north latitude, believed to have been near Nunaksaluk Island, and head for home. He put some finishing touches on his map, and in his journal he wrote:

> Seeing then, that we were practically without anchors and cables that would hold in heavy autumn weather; since we could not be sure of finding good, safe anchorages; since summer was already far advanced and we were in a country where it is always cold, where icebergs are found the whole year round, and where the hills, valleys and the tops of the mountains are always covered with snow, since we were compelled to use our salt for codfish which we had to find elsewhere, and we were 106 leagues away from Belle Isle in a straight line, and at the most fifteen or twenty leagues from the Harbor St. Pierre, and since, moreover, we saw no immediate prospect of meeting Indians with whom we could do enough trade to defray the cost of each day's sailing—we unanimously resolved to find a harbor where we could condition the ship for the return journey to Québec.

On August 16 they headed south down the coast. It had taken him two months and more to reach this point by slow stages, and it was another two months, pausing to catch cod in waters where once again they found these fish plentiful, before he sailed up the St. Lawrence to Mingan to pick up Claire-Françoise and the children. They were delighted to see the sun-browned boys and their father again.

Then they all went to Québec, home for the winter.

20

$\sim\sim\sim\sim\sim$

THE TRIUMPH

THE YEAR BEFORE JOLLIET'S VOYAGE to Labrador, on a gray November day in 1693, when the fogs of the St. Lawrence were closing in so thickly that the pilot could not see where he was going, the ship *Corossol* ran hard on a rock near Seven Islands. So sudden was the impact, so unexpected, that the ship, with a wind behind it, had struck with all its force, and a great hole was crushed in the hull. Water rushed in, and the ship sank so quickly that few passengers or crew had been saved. Pieces of flotsam from the wreck floated in on the tide and drifted around the docks of Québec for days afterward. Now and again the body of a victim washed ashore. For a long time, the wreck of the *Corossol* stayed in the foreground of public attention.

It was a grim and terrible thing. Even to the Canadians, who in their rugged lives in the New World had grown accustomed to terror and the blows of fate against them, were shocked by the wreck.

Louis Jolliet, back in Québec for the winter and making plans for his trip to Labrador the next spring, had heard the news and felt a burning anger against the authorities who permitted such things to happen to innocent people and blundering ships. If the pilot of the *Corossol* had had a good map of the St. Lawrence, had only used the one Jolliet himself had so painstakingly prepared in 1685, fully eight years ago to the day!

It had been on November 10, 1685, that he wrote to Seignelay, minister and secretary of state:

MY LORD:

It is not without reason that from the very beginning ship captains coming to New France have always been apprehensive of the entrance of the Gulf of St. Lawrence and of the navigation from Anticosti to Québec, a distance of more than one hundred and thirty leagues.

It is known, my Lord, that several ships sent by his Majesty as well as by merchants, have been shipwrecked in the said river, for lack of accurate and reliable navigation maps.

Since I completed my studies in philosophy and mathematics eighteen years ago, I have acquired much experience during the voyages I made to the Mississippi River, the Illinois country, the Lake of the Pouteouatami [Green Bay], the country of the Ouenibegons [Winnebago], Lake Superior in the Ottawa country, Baye du Nord [Hudson Bay], Anticosti, Percée Island, Belle Isle and Newfoundland, always with a divider or compass in hand, noting every cape and spit, as well as the bearings from one to the other. This experience emboldens me, my Lord, to present to you this map which is the result of my work during the past six years. You will see marked on it all the coves, islands, and islets, all the coasts and sand bars from Québec to Newfoundland. The pilots of the ships have nothing to fear if they use this map and navigate by it.

I do not hesitate to say that this map is complete, for I inserted in the final draught the information and the noteworthy details observed during 46 voyages on a bark and three in a canoe. Coves and anchorages, good and bad, as well as the bearings, are faithfully entered.

I am not adding the map of the Illinois country, of the Mississippi, or that of the overland route to Hudson Bay, because the maps of these regions which have been sent to his Majesty these past years were all based on my memoirs, and those very enterprises which are now in Canada are the result of the information which I brought back.

Hence it only remained, my Lord, to give you a map of the St. Lawrence River, as accurate and as trustworthy as possible for the navigation of barks and vessels, made by a man with several years' experience. He begs you to accept it as coming from one who considers himself, with all possible respect, my Lord,

Your most humble and obedient servant,

Jolliet

Yes, he had made the navigation map, a chart of utmost accuracy, and if only the King had seen fit to have had copies made of it, so that every ship coming into the St. Lawrence might carry one, and every pilot could study its intricacies and, therefore, bypass the menaces in the river, all would have been well. He wondered what had become of his map. Evidently the King or his minister still had it, and no one had done anything much about the situation. Perhaps they felt, Jolliet mused bitterly at times, that there were others who were better equipped to make maps for King and colonies. There was always the Sieur Franquelin, the foremost hydrographer of the times.

Not until later did Jolliet learn that Denonville had worked in his behalf, though in a somewhat oblique manner which had actually helped Franquelin and not Jolliet.

Denonville had written in November, 1685:

I have had Sieur Franquelin make drawings of Sieur Jolliet's sketches. The latter is seriously interested in his work and has made a thorough study of the river. He has had a great share in many of the discoveries made in this country. He is a good man who could teach navigation and form pilots in this country, if you were kind enough, my Lord, to give him a subsidy each year. The said Jolliet, my Lord, is hoping that his work of the past several years which I have the honor of sending to you, will be rewarded with some pecuniary bounty. He has a fishery at Anticosti, an island which has been granted to him. I am sending in his name a memoir on sedentary fishing to M. Morel, who will speak to you about it. It would be well to employ our Canadians in this occupation. You will see on the map, my Lord, how many settlements there are on both sides of the lower course of the St. Lawrence River.

It was evident from the tone of this letter that the colonial minister and the King believed Canada populated largely by backwoodsmen, trappers, and fishermen, who were mentally unable to accomplish any cultural or scientific contributions for France or America. In writing the above letter, Denonville obviously attempted to give Jolliet a good account, yet ultimately it seemed that he drew more attention to M. Franquelin, who was thereupon, in 1686, given the post of Royal Hydrographer of Québec.

Meanwhile, the colonial minister had sent a M. Deshayes to Canada to survey the river and prepare his own navigation map.

This irritated Denonville. He felt that the minister did not trust his judgment; the news pained Jolliet when he heard of it. It was obvious to him that the King and minister did not trust him, nor any of the Canadians who knew the St. Lawrence far better than the most expert hydrographer from France. To know the river, one must have sailed it almost all of his life, known its currents, its rocks, its islands, and its sudden winds; have known how to calculate a landing when the fog thickened in from the sea; must have known the capes and spits and concealed menaces. This Sieur Deshayes, who was evidently trusted by the King, was no doubt a good mapmaker; but could this man map the St. Lawrence so that a pilot could find his way?

The Sieur Deshayes arrived in Québec in the autumn of 1685, and as soon as the ice broke up in the river the following spring, he would start out on his survey. He insisted to Denonville, however, with some rancor, that he could not do this important work in a mere launch. He would need a bark and a canoe, and a good deal of other equipment and some men. It was going to become an expensive proposition. Denonville, more and more irked, realized that what Deshayes was going to do with such ostentation, had already been done quietly and well by Jolliet. All that needed to be done was for the King and minister to bring themselves to accepting the authority of his expertly drawn map. Yet they had insisted that Franquelin, whom they trusted, redraw Jolliet's "sketches." Now they had sent this pompous Deshayes to do the work over, at untold expense and who knew what accuracy.

Denonville wrote again, veiling his exasperation as well as he could, though it crusted out of his letter like debris rising to the surface of flooding river.

"Our need for maps is most imperative," he wrote. He pleaded that Jolliet be given the job, as well as the position of teacher of navigation in Québec as a reward. He explained also that Deshayes needed a great deal of equipment, and then continued:

> Had I dared, I would have sent back to France the said Sieur Deshayes, because I believe that Sieur Jolliet would have done the work well. However, since you gave orders that Deshayes should come here, I did not think that I should interpret them. Be kind enough, my Lord, to let me know your decision on this matter, and whether, for the survey of the Gulf, you wish to employ Jolliet who owns a bark. . . .

As a clincher, he added: "I am sending an estimate of the expense necessary to equip the bark of Sieur Deshayes, so that you may judge and give the necessary orders."

Denonville, knowing the King's penury when it came to

laying out large sums on the questionable land of New France, pointed out that if Jolliet did the work, he already had a bark of his own; all that the King would be obliged to do for him would give him the job of teacher of navigation in Québec. Whereas, if the expensive Deshayes did the work, the King would have to provide bark, canoe, men, equipment, and a salary as well.

But Denonville was never a very forceful man. He may have had convictions, but, fearing the King might not like them, he was always hesitant in asserting them very strongly. So, although he favored Jolliet, he also did not single him out. He knew that Jolliet wanted to teach navigation, and that he was well fitted for it. But Denonville, in another letter, also proposed the Sieur Franquelin, and it was he who, in 1686, was awarded the post.

Louis accepted what came. He was not a covetous man, though he may have known his moments of anger, impatience, and rebellion. He went out to Anticosti as usual for the fishing. He wished the Sieur Deshayes well, and, since he honestly admired Franquelin's ability as a hydrographer, he did not begrudge him the coveted post. Franquelin, an older man, was honest and highly skilled. Jolliet wished he himself might become as expert in their mutual field, in their great love and fascination for maps. With a whole new world to chart, there was surely room enough for all.

The Sieur Deshayes evidently made his map. But in the November grayness some years later, in 1693, the *Corossol* was wrecked and nearly all lives lost. Evidently the Deshayes map did not work.

Jolliet refused to push himself forward again. It had done so little good before. The King was a hard man to approach with an idea. With some prodding from Frontenac, he had finally come around to giving Jolliet some compensation for his losses to the English in 1690, but as yet had done nothing about helping him after the attack on Mingan.

When the news of the *Corossol* reached France by the first ship in the following spring, Pontchartrain, the colonial minister, shocked into action, wrote at once to Frontenac and Champigny to exert themselves anew and see that everything in their power was done to assure safe navigation of the river and the Gulf of St. Lawrence, and to have the whole thing remapped in such a way that pilots could follow with assurance and safety.

There was a good deal of correspondence between Frontenac and Champigny in Canada, and the King and Pontchartrain in France. The King and his minister were putting the blame on the Canadians for the wreck of the *Corossol* and the failure of navigation aids, while Frontenac and Champigny, fearful of their skins, were trying to place the blame elsewhere.

Frontenac wrote:

> If His Majesty would kindly take care of the necessary expenses, we could certainly find here a man who could acquire a thorough knowledge of the river, if he were to devote his full attention to this during one summer. This would be more useful than all that has been done thus far. We shall do our best to have Sieur Jolliet and others who sail this river, make a full report of all they know about it.

The year was 1695 when the King wrote again to Frontenac and Champigny. The letter bore a reproving and somewhat irritable tone, as if Louis XIV were growing very tired of the minor bothers of the colony, wondering why his officers there could not take care of their business themselves.

The King urged Frontenac and Champigny to insist that those in the colony who had a greater experience than these two, pool their knowledge, redraw the maps, and have them sent with all haste to Paris, so that those maps which were already at hand could be corrected and completed. Yes, the King knew about the Sieur Jolliet. He had but lately received the latter's Labrador map. His Majesty was therefore returning the petition presented in his behalf so that Frontenac and Champigny might report on what reasonable provision could be made in the matter. But, said the King, ending his letter on a sudden note of hope and favor: "To encourage him [Jolliet] his Majesty is willing, if they think proper, to give him some bonus from the war budget."

And so at last there was official sanction. Frontenac and Champigny hastily hired Jolliet to map the St. Lawrence. They paid him 675 livres for what he had done in the past; payment for the new map was yet to come.

Louis Jolliet had no time to spend in rejoicing. In that same month of November, 1695, two years after the *Corossol* was wrecked, a ship named the *Charente*, delayed by storms at sea, belatedly limped up the river to Québec. The *Charente* was obliged to get back to France before winter, and winter was already upon the land. The captain was fearful of attempting it. His pilot refused point-blank to go. It was not the open sea they feared, but the hazards of the river and the gulf.

Louis had come home to the house on the Rue Sous-le-Fort and was comfortable before the fire. The children had run in from school as dusk moved with chill purple-gray shadows early over the streets of Québec. Charles and François had walked down the steep incline of Mountain Hill from the seminary. Claire-Françoise and the girls were preparing the evening meal, with Marie Lalande's help, when the messenger came to the door with a letter for Jolliet.

As he read, his excitement grew. He called the family together to listen to what had happened—and who knew what else might not develop from this one event!

The ship *Charente* had to depart two days hence, and there was no pilot to take the vessel from Québec to the sea. The weather was bad, the river treacherous, and the French pilot, though he had brought the ship in safely enough, had become too nervous and unsure of himself to navigate back again. The best pilot in Canada would be needed if the *Charente* were to sail. And Louis Jolliet was said to be the best, assured Champigny in the letter. He had been chosen, if he would go, leaving his business and his family for the winter, for there would be no coming back after the ship gained the open sea. He would have to stay aboard and go all the way to France with the *Charente*, stay the winter, and return on the first vessel heading westward in the spring.

This was his chance. He would, personally, take his maps to the King, would talk to Louis XIV in his palace, if he could gain permission, or, if not, then with My Lord Pontchartrain. He would show him the maps, tell him what needed to be done for the safe navigation of Canada's waters. Since the poor Sieur Franquelin's family had been lost in a shipwreck not long before, on their way to join him in Canada, and in grief he had gone back to France to take care of his affairs there, perhaps the position so long coveted by Jolliet would be open again.

Claire-Françoise had not expected her husband to go away again so soon. He usually stayed in Québec during the winter. He was the regular organist at the Cathedral of Notre Dame and sometimes assisted with the music at the seminary.

Jolliet had never lost his love for music. When he was troubled, he could go to the quiet chapel, with only the votive lights flickering gently, and the Blessed Virgin smiling sweetly down at him, the altar serene and full of faith, and the presence of God all about, and play softly on the organ. The music would swell louder and more powerfully as his emotions rose, as he combated the discontent of his soul, his worries of providing for his family now that they had lost so much to the English. France had not reimbursed him nearly enough to pay back what he had lost. He had made the Labrador trip, with little enough monetary gain, though with great profit to his own adventurous soul in seeing new lands, new people, and in making one of his maps, one of the things, next to playing the organ, which he most loved doing.

The organ tones would sink lower, then, in minor key, mourning for what he would have been and might have done, if he had been able; longing, sometimes, secretly, as only the Blessed Virgin knew, and had surely forgiven him for it, for the Illinois country to which he had never been able to return. The music did much for him; it was a spiritual pleasure which he also derived from playing for the masses all winter long.

He would have to miss it this winter. He would be in France. He wished, perhaps, that he could take Claire-Françoise. She would marvel at the sights, but, like him, perhaps she would be eager to get back to the better life, the safer life, the calmer life, along the St. Lawrence, where the perfume of the northern forests, the winds from the south, and the odors of the sea and the river filled the air.

Claire-Françoise bade him farewell, and the younger children clung to him as he kissed them all several times around, and embraced his tall, grown sons. He was especially sorry to miss being in Québec this winter, for the first member of the family to leave its circle, Marie-Geneviève, was going to be married in the early spring. He felt sure that he could never get back in time to attend the wedding, though he would return on the very first ship to leave France.

When he came back, perhaps something would have happened in France, on the King's own doorstep, which would help him give his family more means and security. He could not always depend upon the Sieur de La Chesnaye, who for so many years had come to the rescue of the Jolliets when they were in need of something. He had underwritten new supplies for rebuilding the Anticosti and Mingan houses and warehouses. He had always been generous and willing, but Louis wished to reach a point of being completely independent of his beneficence. La Chesnaye was his uncle, but he had always disliked Claire-Françoise. There had been for years an unexpressed but evident enmity which increased rather than lessened with time. Louis loved his uncle; but he preferred not to rely upon him. He wanted to secure his own financial independence in case death took him early and left Claire-Françoise to La Chesnaye's cold mercy.

Louis Jolliet felt certain that what he had hoped for from the King would materialize from this trip. He had been told of the contents of the letter which was being sent with him. Frontenac and Champigny, writing jointly to the King, as they so often did—perhaps for greater strength in standing together against the wrath of Louis XIV, and hiding behind each other's iniquities, though they disliked each other cordially, said:

> We could not give him [the captain of the *Charente*] a better pilot than Sieur Jolliet who is perhaps the only one in this country capable of acquitting himself well of this task. I am very much pleased that he should have the opportunity of presenting his maps to you in person, and of telling you of his discoveries; and I shall be very much pleased if you will do him all the favors you can.

Later they wrote to Pontchartrain, adding, that because this assignment given to Jolliet "will force him to go to

France, we did not think we could give him less than 600
livres, seeing that he leaves his family and abandons his
trade and his enterprises. We believe, my Lord, that you
will approve of what we have done." Still later, Frontenac
and Champigny suggested that Jolliet be appointed to the
position of hydrographer at Québec, until lately held by
Sieur Franquelin.

And so Louis Jolliet sailed with the tide. With the
Charente's decks under him and the rigging singing in a
brisk November wind, he piloted the ship expertly out the
channel past the Île d'Orléans, past the Gaspé shore and
the winds of Matane, across to enter the Détroit de Jacques
Cartier; past Anticosti; turning a little southeast to pass
through the Cabot Strait between Newfoundland and Nova
Scotia; and into the Atlantic at last.

With the heaving gray waters and mists of the Atlantic
safely under the hull of the *Charente*, the captain breathed a
sigh of deep relief, while Louis Jolliet, who had had no qualms,
settled down to enjoy the rest of the long voyage to France.
It was a rough trip; this was the stormy time of year. Usually
the last ships from Québec had long since gone before this
time. It was January when the *Charente* at last landed at
the quay at La Rochelle, and Louis, with his maps and small
baggage, stepped ashore into the wind and snow.

While he was in France, he evidently was favorably
received by the King and the minister, Lord Pontchartrain,
though there are no specific records of the meeting nor of
what went on in the elegant quarters of the Sun King and
the august minister. Nevertheless, when Louis sailed for
home on the first ship, he carried with him the long-coveted
commission of Royal Hydrographer, the King's Map Maker
of Québec. He was, besides, to teach hydrography.

At the same time he delivered mail to Frontenac and

Champigny which did not especially cheer them. Old Frontenac, often ailing and growing more crotchety and difficult to get along with, felt that it was hardly worth while these days to get letters from France. They contained so little news that was inspiriting or even pleasant.

Frontenac had been thoroughly discouraged by the royal edict which had just come from the King, forbidding him to grant any more leaves of absence, or congés. It seemed that nothing he did, he complained to the equally discouraged and gloomy Champigny, was ever right in the eyes of the King and his minister. They were impossible to please. If they were only here for a while in this rough land, they could see what he was up against. . . .

Therefore, he felt that Jolliet was particularly lucky to have received his commission.

Frontenac wrote: "We are living in a time so little propitious for obtaining favors that it is much that Jolliet should have obtained the position of professor of hydrography."

Frontenac, perhaps, was even a trifle envious, though he could not deny that Jolliet deserved his honors at last.

Frontenac and Champigny, feeling that Jolliet should have something for all his services, now that the King at last was acknowledging him, gave him a small tract of valuable land on the Etchamin River, on the south side of the St. Lawrence opposite Québec and Sillery.

Jolliet opened his school of hydrography in Québec. He taught pilots and mapmakers during the winter, but still spent the summers at Anticosti or at Mingan or at Seven Islands, carrying on a busy life in trade and fishing.

The land grant on the Etchamin River was Frontenac's final favor to Louis Jolliet. As the early winter of 1698 drew over Québec, Frontenac lay ill in the Chateau St. Louis. Daily he grew weaker. Then on November 28, the solemn bells of the churches of Québec and Montréal and in all the little parishes along the river from Tadoussac to the Ottawa River began to toll. Louis Buade, the Count de Frontenac, was dead.

The old man, in spite of his often underhanded dealings and his difficulty in getting along with certain people of authority, was mourned throughout the land he had loved. Jolliet was in Québec when it happened. He was beginning work on a navigation map of Cabot Straits when word came. When he heard the bells tolling, he laid down his pen, and went at once to the cathedral. His world, he felt, would never be the same again, not without the militant, exciting Frontenac bellowing and loving and cajoling and fighting to preserve French Canada. An era had ended as the century itself neared its close.

That winter Louis completed his new map of the St. Lawrence and the Cabot Straits—the map which the *Corossol* should have had, the one which, if the pilot of the *Charente* had used it, could have taken him safely out to the open sea.

Life was good. Louis Jolliet felt an expansion of comfort and well-being. He had a busy career in the kind of work he loved, a contented existence with his family, none of whom save pretty Marie-Geneviève had as yet left for separate establishments of their own. His abilities at last were recognized, and he had a chance to make the expert maps and charts which he knew so well how to draw. Slowly once more he was beginning to build up a small, but growing, financial backlog. With his work at the school his winters were full. When the summer came, he and his family went once more out to the open waters and to the fragrant spruce country and the fogs and birds of Anticosti Island.

21

~~~~~~~~~

THE NORTHERN MYSTERY

THE NORTH WOULD ALWAYS HOLD ITS MYSTERY for Louis
Jolliet. Unyielding of all its secrets to any man, closing its
life securely under ice and stinging snow of the long, long
winter, the north would never tell him all he wanted to
know. Perhaps it would tell no man, ever. Perhaps man in
his unrest would go on, always wondering what lay beyond
the next island, the next bay, the next horizon, and continuing to find that still more islands, more bays, and more
horizons lay beyond. A man, however, could always hope
and dream.

It was his hope and his dreams and his inner courage
which would lead him beyond discouragement, beyond the
defeat of one man or one nation or of one generation, to
find his solution to his own life as well as to the mysteries
of the world. He, Jolliet, had not solved the northern mystery, had not found the route to the Pacific. Perhaps the
only way to find a short cut to that elusive ocean would be
to cut a canal through the narrow isthmus where Balboa
once stood, to connect Atlantic with Pacific at Panama. He
did not know. But always there was the challenge: and there
might even be a route connecting Atlantic with Pacific by
way of the north—somewhere. Not by way of the Mississippi;
he had solved that puzzle. Not by way of Lake Superior;

236

he had decided against that. Perhaps Hudson Bay and the Arctic Sea were the key. Perhaps the only way in which a man could go from sea to sea across the north would be to swim like a seal under the ice! Jolliet could laugh when he thought of that. No man, perhaps, might ever solve the northern mystery.

When his school was dismissed in June, 1700, he was glad to get away from Québec. He loaded his bark with books and foodstuffs and clothes for his family for three months' stay on Anticosti. He had trade goods for the Indians. It should be a profitable summer. Claire-Françoise, Jean-Baptiste, and Claire went along; perhaps the older boys accompanied their parents to work with their father in the fisheries. Marie-Geneviève, married, stayed with her husband and child. The family set off with the servants for the Gulf of St. Lawrence.

It was a sparkling, unseasonably warm day as the ship waited in the harbor for the final loading. There was a buoyant air of delight at the coming holiday, at escaping from the city streets and the cramped view. Looking at the city, both in the lower parts and on the heights, Louis could remember how much changed it was from the time he stood on the deck of the ship which brought him for the first time to France, that year when he had left the seminary. He could remember something of how it had been in his boyhood, too, a dismal sort of place at times, filled with an air of discouragement and squalor. Now it was a bustling town with many beautiful stone houses and public buildings, with the Chateau St. Louis visible as an imposing mass at the top of the bluff, and the cannons half seen around the ramparts as a warning against the English not to come again. He could feel a swelling pride in his city, especially when he stood off from it and observed its splendor.

The ship was readied. The sails were up, the lines untied, the anchor raised, and the summer wind carried the bark quickly away from the city on the great gray rock. The family disposed themselves about the ship, while Louis, at the helm, conducted his trim ship down the widening course of the St. Lawrence.

Québec never saw him again. If anyone knew what happened out there on the wild Gulf of St. Lawrence and in the wilderness of Anticosti where the sea birds coasted past all day and seals sunned themselves on the rocks, no one told.

For Louis Jolliet perished that summer. Perhaps it was time for him to go.

As far as known history is concerned, he simply vanished from the life of the world. Claire-Françoise, who was left in near poverty when the debts were paid, evidently did not tell the details, nor did his sons and daughters and kinsmen, of whom he had many. Louis Jolliet by 1700 was a noted man . . . but no one knows where he was buried, nor why nor how he died. Perhaps he did indeed lose his life in the sea or in the river, and his body was never recovered. Perhaps . . .

The old, faded writing in a parish priest's records in the Cathedral of Notre Dame in Québec merely states:

1700, September 15, a service for the deceased M. Jolliet in recognition of his having played the organ at the cathedral and parish during many years. Given gratis.

BIBLIOGRAPHY

Costain, Thomas B. *The White and the Gold: The French Regime in Canada.* New York: Doubleday & Co., 1954.

Dean, Sidney W., with Marguerite Mooers Marshall. *We Fell in Love with Quebec.* Philadelphia: Macrae Smith Co., 1950.

De La Roche, Mazo. *Quebec, Historic Seaport.* New York: Doubleday & Co., 1944.

Delanglez, Jean. *Louis Jolliet: 1645–1700.* Jesuit Institute, 1943.

Deuel, Thorne. *Hopewellian Communities of Illinois.* Illinois State Museum, Scientific Papers, Vol. V. 1952.

Rutledge, Joseph Lister. *Century of Conflict.* New York: Doubleday & Co., 1956.

Steck, Francis Borgia. *The Jolliet-Marquette Expedition.* Franciscan Fathers, Quincy, Illinois.

Temple, Wayne C. *Indian Villages of the Illinois Country.* Illinois State Museum. Scientific Papers, Vol. II, part 2. 1958.

Tucker, Sara Jones. *Indian Villages of the Illinois Country,* reproductions of old maps. Illinois State Museum, Scientific Papers, Vol. II, part 1. 1948.

INDEX